Five Loaves
and
Two Fishes

New Life Through Inner Healing

Phoebe Cranor

Paulist Press ◆ New York ◆ Mahwah

Library of Congress Cataloging-in-Publication Data

Cranor, Phoebe.
    Five loaves and two fishes.

      1. Christian life—1960—   . 2. Cranor,
Phoebe. I. Title. II. Title. 5 loaves and
2 fishes.
BV4501.2.C725   1987   248.4   87–2342
ISBN 0-8091-2881-0 (pbk.)

Published by Paulist Press
997 Macarthur Boulevard
Mahwah, New Jersey 07430

Printed and bound in the
United States of America

Contents

Introduction

It was a beautiful clear summer day high in the mountains. We had eaten our picnic lunch at the edge of a lake where not a breath of wind moved even a leaf, and the smooth water religiously reflected every mountain and blade of grass. Everyone else had gone for a hike or fishing, but I sat, quiet, on the smooth stone trying to overcome a mood of depression.

"There's so much needing to be done," I thought glumly. "I feel as if I am alone and helpless, and what little I manage to accomplish doesn't make a dent in the needs and demands of the world." I tried to pray. How can a person pray for the nebulous "lots to be done" that I was feeling? "Lord, help!"

A bird flew out over the still water and, by the natural process of elimination, dropped a small white blob which fell with a plop into the quiet lake. Entranced, I watched as ring after ring moved toward the shore. At my feet, finally, came the minute lap-lap which made its own mark where the rocks had once been dry. The bird had given only what he no longer needed—but even his discard had changed, for at least a few seconds, the shoreline of the mountain lake. I picked up my Bible.

"Looking up, Jesus saw the crowds approaching and said to Philip, 'Where can we buy some bread for these people to eat?' He only said this to test Philip; he himself knew exactly what he was going to do. Philip answered, 'Two hundred denarii would only buy enough to give them a small piece each.' One of his disciples, Andrew, Simon Pe-

1

ter's brother, said, 'There is a small boy here with five barley loaves and two fish; but what is that for so many?' Jesus said to them, 'Make the people sit down.' There was plenty of grass there, and as many as five thousand men sat down. Then Jesus took the loaves, gave thanks, and gave them out to all who were sitting ready; he then did the same with the fish, giving out as much as was wanted. When they had eaten enough he said to the disciples, 'Pick up the pieces left over, so that nothing gets wasted.' So they picked them up, and filled twelve hampers with scraps left over from the meal of five barley loaves. The people, seeing this sign that he had given, said, 'This really is the prophet who is to come into the world' " (Jn 6:5–15).

I have read that then, as now, barley was the poor man's bread material. The wealthy had wheat flour. The little boy had nothing special for his lunch. Small hard barley bread and boiled fish are not the repast of a king. But the child gave what he had—all he had, no matter how poor it might have seemed. And the Lord Jesus took what was offered and turned it into a miracle. The waves of movement flowed in circles around the miracle forever. Five small hard barley loaves and two little boiled fish have become a never-ending motion toward eternity because one unknown child offered Jesus his lunch. I looked at the smooth lake and felt its calm flowing through me. All I had to do was give the Lord whatever I had: my own five poor-man's cakes and my two little bites of protein. All, did I say? Have you ever tried to give away all you have? I have fear, sins, regrets, pride, judgment, anger, prejudice, unforgiveness. I have sorrows. I have mistakes. I have hurts from my past and empty spaces, holes inside of me filled with longing and need. Five loaves? Well, I might have five hundred. But are they of any value? The disciples asked, "What is that among so many?" I might well ask, "Are they anything but trash?" Still, the bird's small visceral discard did change the shoreline of a vast mountain lake.

"All right, Lord Jesus, I'll try. If I can bear to look at all my trash myself, I'll give it to you and see how many of the five thousand you can feed. It seems hopeless to me. Nevertheless, not my will, but thine, be done. Amen."

1

THE FIRST BARLEY LOAF: ANGER

Once when I was a child, we visited some friends upstream from an artesian well. I was absolutely fascinated by the way the water bubbled and spewed. When the wind blew, it splashed over rocks and grass, bending the flowers down, splattering the visiting butterflies. I watched it for hours. Then one day the owner of the pasture from which it flowed decided it was causing too much mud and making a slough of his land. So he put a tight cap over it.

"Where did the water go?" I asked him.

"Oh, it's still under there," he answered. "It'll come up somewhere else downstream from here."

Sure enough, next time I visited there was a fresh bubbling spring (with or without his permission) down in the neighbor's pasture. Years later when I returned to the valley, I was disappointed. The lovely, artistic artesian wells had all been capped with pipelines and were busily watering gardens of carrots and turnips and onions and potatoes. What had once been a land of alternating arid hillsides and marshes full of cattails was now neat rows of produce with a fleet of trucks hauling their piles of vegetables to market. Perhaps what I looked at as the romance of the free-flowing springs was gone, but I had to admit that the result of the water's use was admirable.

A memory of those fascinating artesian wells tipped me off about my first barley loaf to offer my Savior. In our fallen condition, our imperfection and our sinfulness, "I love you because I need you" seems to be the most usual and popular definition of love. We do need each other in many ways, most of them subtle. My mother was the oldest in a large family and she never had much she could claim for her own. She needed for me to be *hers.* She was reluctant to share me with even my father. She kept me at home and protected me as much as possible from any contact with the outside world. She liked to have me ill so she could spend her whole attention on me, and of course she alienated what few friends I managed to make. She often told me how much she loved me—how she would simply die if anything happened to me. I understand now. I know the depth of her own deprivation and her own needs. But as a child, I did not feel loved, no matter how emphatically mother declared her affection. As I look back on my feelings, I see that the predominant awareness of my childhood was that I was a possession to be used. Of course, I didn't identify it as such at the time. When I was told, "Oh you know you don't think that. I won't have you thinking that way," or "You really don't feel that way, you know. Mother knows how you really feel," I was only confused. The confusion was hidden deep down, pressed away because there was no way for me to deal with it. A child's mother is the figure around which his life revolves. What mother says *must* be the truth. Somehow I *must* conform to whatever she has told me. Although my poor mother assured me often and vehemently that she loved me, I was never convinced.

But deep inside, where I put all things for safe-keeping, I was storing up a reservoir of anger. My subconscious awareness of my true person would not accept someone else's evaluation of my emotions. In fact, my subconscious was furious. In my house, though, nobody ever expressed anger. To be angry was automatically to have every profession or expression of love immediately pulled away. "Nice girls do *not* act like that." And only "nice" girls were loved. With the already present confusion about being loved permeating every part of my personality, the risk was too great. I learned never to allow anyone to know when I was angry—not even myself. Some people's artesian wells bubble all over everything. Mine was capped in no uncertain terms. It moved into different pastures and made ugly mudholes there, but I didn't understand what was happening for a long time. In fact, I didn't see the light until I was able to offer the whole mess to the Lord.

I made a child's commitment to Jesus when I was seven. Of course I spent a great deal of time doing the usual intellectual exploration of the meaning of his Gospel and "deciding" how I was going to live. Then one day I had a personal encounter with the living Lord which changed all my intellectualizing into love for him. I began to read the Bible with enthusiasm for more information about my new-found Savior. It was at that point I sat on the shore of the mountain lake and thought about my five small barley loaves and my two little boiled fishes. There was no doubt that barley loaf number one had to be the tremendous supply of buried anger I was beginning to suspect lay somewhere in the depths of me. But anger was "bad!" It was a "no-no!" Could I even look at it myself, let alone offer it to Jesus?

We have been taught to do many things with our anger: repress it, deny it, feel guilty about it. Nobody I ever knew had looked at it as something worthy of deliberately holding up as a gift. Still, God did make anger. Jesus expressed it. I was astounded when I discovered the number of times he was openly angry. Somehow I must see my anger honestly and evaluate it with a clear head.

One cold, cloudy day, I was lying on the floor by the heat register looking at a catalogue full of household gadgets. In it I found a picture of a thing you were to lay in the skillet when frying an egg. It made the egg turn out square to fit into a sandwich. As I looked at it, I felt a surge of inner tearfulness. "Poor egg!" I wailed, without thinking.

Now logic would surely insist that, if an egg had feelings at all, they would be hurt more by being fried than by being square. My emotional response to the shape of the egg was a key to my own inner fury at someone's efforts to change my natural personality: the self-image with which I was born. I lay there on the carpet, trying to laugh at myself and failing completely. Finally, in desperation, I cried aloud, "Lord Jesus, what *is* the matter with me today?"

As I uttered the words, I had a mental picture of a large cannister full of pencils with the points broken off. There was nothing more, and I had no idea what the picture meant. But as I looked at the pencils, I realized, finally, that I was very angry—deep and boiling like the artesian well.

"Give in to it. Acknowledge it. Act on it," the Lord seemed to say. So I did, tentatively at first and then with more and more vigor. I pounded my fists on the floor and screamed. My words surprised me so much that I sat up in disbelief. It was the first time I had ever identified my basic pain in terms I could speak aloud.

"Mother, why do I need to be changed? Am I not all right as I am? Why do I have to be the way *you* want me to be?" I had addressed my mother as if she were in the room with me. I had expressed for the first time my primal fury. I was shaking with long-unacknowledged tension.

The presence of the Lord Jesus came into the room, and as he said so often to those about him in Palestine long ago, he repeated to me: "Do not be afraid."

"How can I help it?" I sobbed, snuggling into the comfort of his presence. The answer to that question has been forthcoming for several years since I first asked it. Now I know several things I can do with my anger. But first, before anything else, I must hand it, as did the boy on the shore of the lake, to Jesus and see what use *he* can make of it.

And how do I "hand it to Jesus"? After all, our Lord on the shores of the Sea of Galilee was a flesh and blood person into whose solid hands the little boy could lay his lunch. He could feel the food and the warmth of the hands that took it. I had given my life to the Lord but how was I to give him my anger? "Tell me, Lord," I prayed, "how to give you this meager, none-too-tasty offering."

Prayer isn't always simply words. Sometimes it is pictures and sensations and awareness. Sometimes it is emotions. As I prayed for wisdom about my gift of anger, I began to see in my mind my own hands, full of a lumpy solid chunk of dark bread. They lifted it up and the hands of my Lord reached down to accept it. As I saw them holding it tenderly, warmth and peace flowed over me. Before I could

10

move, though, even in my imagination, I felt him smiling his thanks for what I had done.

As I made the gesture, the first frightening time, to offer my rage to Jesus, a picture of the rest of his story came into my mind. Before he did anything else with the child's food, he blessed it and, the other Gospels say, *broke* it into pieces. My cannister of blunted pencils was showing me that I had dulled the points my anger was making—the pointers to areas that must first be broken before they could become a blessing. Maybe if I looked at each surge of inner anger, it would aim me in the direction of a solid mass untouched by the gentleness of the Master's hands.

I am quite sure that inside every person is the map of his own perfection and wholeness which God put there in the beginning. When Jesus said, "You must therefore be perfect just as your heavenly Father is perfect" (Mt 5:48), he must have meant just what he said: not to *act* perfect or *pretend* perfection, but to *be* perfect. And what is perfection if it is not wholeness? Nobody can achieve his own wholeness, I'm positive. However, he gave us the command, and it is he himself who has been offered to help our growth in that direction. All we have to do is give him permission to take whatever we have of imperfection and work on it his own way. It's the giving that's hard. As with my anger, I have my own ideas about it. Most of them came from my childhood and are not necessarily valid. But they are mine, and I tend to hang onto them right along with the anger itself.

The first dull pencil I took to the holy pencil-sharpener and had worked over was the one which pointed to a misconception: "It is wrong to *be* angry." In my family it was wrong, but in God's eyes it seems not to be. Scripture openly deals with the fact of Jesus' fury with hypocrisy, lack of love, misuse of God's holiness, and such other manifestations of his real, human feelings. He was angry with misdeeds and non-love even while he could love and forgive the mis-doer and the non-lover. Jesus offered us a picture of the nature of God, and I must accept that the "wrath of

God" is a very real and necessary part of his nature. I must know that God loves me and forgives me for my possible *mis-use* of my anger and that the anger itself is there because he created me so in the beginning. I finally began to see that everyone has a little spring of normal and natural anger flowing out of him for the purpose of righting wrongs and unseating evil. It is only when it is denied and dammed off that it becomes a dangerous reservoir. The artesian well was a perfectly natural phenomenon. Capped, it exploded; piped it became productive. In its free-flowing state, that bubbling water might cause discomfort. Natural and unchanneled, it had the propensity of making a swamp.

"In everyday life, then, Lord Jesus, what do I do about anger?" I asked. "No matter where it came from, if I am to offer my little cake for a subsequent miracle, then I want to know how. The words 'just hand it to you' are too lofty. I want some practical help."

Into my waiting consciousness came an awareness stronger than words. I must allow myself to *know* whenever I am angry. Perhaps that would be easy for some people to accomplish. But when one has been given the message over and over in all sorts of subtle ways that he is not *ever* to feel anger, the only way to manage one's behavior is to deny to himself that the feelings were ever present in the first place. Otherwise the inner world would be one of unending conflict. I managed very successfully. My image of myself was of a person so calm and unruffled that nothing ever upset me. On the surface I could act out the image most of the time, but inside I was as ruffled as a pinafore. All sorts of things upset me. Without the personal presence of Jesus, I never dared to start looking at my honest feelings for fear they would immediately begin scattering themselves all over the place.

But now I had a new choice. I must acknowledge my rage quickly, and consciously, with determination, hand it to Jesus.

Trying to give my anger to Jesus, though, presumed

that I trusted his love and his plans for me. My original experience with the reality of his wonderful caring had convinced me that I would always afterward trust him. To my horror, I discovered that such might not be the case. Part of me had never learned to trust love, even that of the Lord. The only honest course I could take, it seemed, was to will to trust, whether I did or not, and be open to whatever changes would subsequently occur. Putting my eyes on myself and my progress toward accomplishing wholeness and perfection was no more effective than a continual pulling up of the turnips to see if they were growing. Even when I finally began to come to terms with the extent of my inner anger, I still didn't really know how to give it to my Lord. Somehow there had to be a way for me to lose my self-centeredness and allow wholeness to happen without constant frantic effort. It seemed to me this first small barley loaf was going to give me a lot of trouble before the miracle of brokenness and multiplication could take place.

"I do love you, Lord," I prayed. "I know I don't love you and trust you enough, but I have met you in person and I want to give you everything inside of me to do with as you will. Please help me." That was an honest prayer, and almost immediately he began to answer it. He did it his own way, though, and not with the instantaneous results I anticipated. And he did make me help—not frantically, maybe, or fearfully, but steadily and hard. My wholeness apparently is a joint operation undertaken in the beginning by my Creator, but he is quietly waiting for me to will to participate. Free choice is, I guess, the most special and at the same time the most difficult of the characteristics of human beings. What a chance he took when God gave it to us! He forced himself, by that one miracle, to have to provide us with hell in case that was our chosen option.

My part was to continue to deliberately choose faith over fear; to continue to acknowledge each moment of anger, no matter how tiny, and to determinedly will to trust him as he dealt with it; to take the one step past my own

13

awareness of his love and choose to believe even when I had no such feelings; and, best of all, to read Scripture with the specific objective of finding how often God our Father told his people that he loved them. The Bible is full of the message. I didn't know it, and I'm sure many others don't either. We often read it as rules or as history. How often do we read it as a love letter from a caring Father? "Because he loved your fathers and chose their descendants after them, he brought you out of Egypt, openly showing his presence and his great power" (Dt 4:37). Because he loves the whole of mankind, he will bring me out of my private Egypt and give me freedom. And right along with the message of his love comes the message that I must deepen my own love for him. The Old Testament says, "You shall love Yahweh your God with all your heart, with all your soul, and with all your strength" (Dt 6:4—5). The New Testament says that Jesus repeated this commandment. It is an imperative—and I had to put it into practice.

I began to work with the techniques I was seeing. I began to recognize every surge of anger at the time—and not two weeks later, as I had done for years. I began to give it, with cheerful deliberation, into the hands of Jesus; I worked at expressing with my mouth and believing in my heart that he accepted my emotion because he loved me and was willing to heal me. And I did some contemplated reprogramming of my feelings toward God the Father, God the Son, and my constant helper, the Holy Spirit. I did it, did I say? I only offered my own weakness, and he was responsible for both the will and the action that took place. But, still, there was more to this first barley cake than I anticipated.

Anger was its basic ingredient. But along with it were the guilt at openly acknowledging an "unacceptable" emotion and the fear that must be the underground river out of which the artesian spring might be bubbling. With my hand in the Lord's and my focus glued to him for support, I began carefully to take apart every surge of fury. A gift to Jesus, in my life at least, can never be a simple blanket, "Take my all."

Over and over, he seems to make me look at what I have, and, before giving it to him, understand it myself.

Each time I looked long and hard enough at a spurt of anger, I could see an underlying fear. Most often it was the fear that somebody had set about to reshape me like a wad of modeling clay instead of letting me develop as my own insides were demanding. Several times I found myself coming back to the basic "primal scream" of my childhood: "What is wrong with me the way I am? Why are you trying to change me?" My recurring and frightening dream for years and years had always been that I was about to be run over by a steamroller. I would jump wildly, usually really leaping out of bed onto the floor with subsequent bruises and abrasions. My subconscious knew that I was in constant danger of having my original design damaged, and the dream was a graphic description of my inner awareness. Being run over by a steamroller does have a tendency to alter one's shape. My subconscious understood. So I jumped and was safe again—until the next night.

Giving the anger and its concurrent fear to the Savior finally began to become a habit. Over and over I offered each tiny grain of barley to Jesus, often with embarrassment and psychic discomfort. And again and again I talked to myself about giving up the guilty feelings that insisted upon arising whenever I expressed "unjustified" anger. The process was discouragingly slow, and many times a day I found myself praying "Help, Lord Jesus."

"Lo, I am with you always," came to me at every crisis, comforting and encouraging me. Obviously we were in the "miracle" together, he and I, and I must keep working at my end of the task. Finally it became obvious to me that the only option I had was to use anger of any kind as a pointer to direct my attention to the Lord Jesus and God the Father, and to constantly ask the help of the Spirit. The blunted pencils began to have points. They pointed to my need to "seek first the kingdom" and the King in charge of the kingdom.

Verses for Prayer

Jesus said, "I am the light of the world; anyone who follows me will not be walking in the dark; he will have the light of life" (Jn 8:12).

Paul said, "I am quite certain that the one who began this good work in you will see that it is finished when the Day of Christ Jesus comes" (Phil 1:6).

The Miracle of Freedom

Once I took a long walk. Usually I like to walk, but this particular time I kept feeling more and more tired, distracted, and cross. The scenery was lovely; the path was smooth; the wind was cool and the sunshine caressing. There were birds in the trees and flowers in bloom all along the edges of my pathway. Butterflies decorated the horizon. But I didn't notice. I was too caught up in my own feelings of discomfort. Finally I stopped, sat down on a rock, and took stock of the situation. It was at that moment that I discovered the source of my utter lack of enthusiasm for my beautiful walk. There was a burr in my sock. It had rubbed against my ankle until blood oozed into the cloth, but I had not even been aware of its presence. I don't know why I didn't notice it, unless it was because I had taught myself not to acknowledge the things which bothered me. In any case, I sat down and pulled out the burr. All of a sudden the footpath became beautiful. I could hear the birds. I could feel the softly moving air and see the butterflies. It was as if the removal of a small, insignificant seed-pod had utterly transformed the countryside. The miracle of the first barley loaf was beginning to happen.

As the habit of recognizing anger and offering it to Jesus solidified, that old, old burr came loose from my sock and allowed me a new kind of personal freedom. And more than a useless burr, the anger soon became a productive tool. As the memory of my old friend, the artesian well, came again to mind, I could see that Jesus was indeed using that ever-present, bubbling emotion for watering the arid landscape. Where the original fury immobilized me, the newly dedicated feeling seemed to energize me. I became more interested in other people and less concerned with myself. Instead of becoming angry at a person who had hurt me, I began to be angry at the circumstances which created in him the need to be cruel. I began to be aware of his inner needs and pain, and so was able to be compassionate and to pray for him.

A community in love was truly beginning to emerge. As an "only," I had always been a shy child, afraid of relationships. My lack of experience with them had made it hard for me to be free in any sort of group. Besides, I was always afraid I would show anger at some crucial point and be forever banished from the love of others. With Jesus holding that dangerous commodity in *his* hands, though, it became easier to love and trust my friends. I started carefully, but at least I made some genuine moves toward community. Scar tissue from past unhealed anger separates and divides us, but healing softens us toward one another. Jesus said that outsiders would recognize his followers by the love they had for one another. Slowly but surely I am learning what he meant.

Jesus was—and still is—the only completely perfect person: perfect beacause he is one person of the Trinity. I used to wonder how he could see so well into each person's needs, know so well what to do for every situation, love and care for even those who hated and rejected him. It was because he had no need to worry about and protect his own hurting insides. He had no burr in his sock; he was free to be altogether present to every other person simply because he had no inner demand to keep part of himself present to care for his own needs. I am beginning to appreciate Paul's understanding of what happens to us when we invite Jesus into our lives—when we give him our unlovely little barley cakes. Colossians 3:10 says, "You have stripped off your old behavior with your old self, and you have put on a new self which will *progress* toward true knowledge the more it is renewed in the image of its Creator." Take my anger, Lord, and help me to grow into the image of my Creator. There's a lot yet to do, but I feel as if I have started at least.

Soon after beginning my project of giving my loaves and fishes to Jesus, I became a member of a small group of women who pray for the wholeness of themselves and others. We intercede for the obvious gaps where Jesus' love is missing and a section of a person's life is not filled out, or where, as it was with my anger, pressure is present like a capped artesian well waiting to explode. We pray that the emptiness will be filled or the pressure will be removed, and we are available for whoever wishes to participate with us. It was surprising how often hidden anger surfaced at our meetings. One day a young woman came to us asking for help with her relationship with her husband. He had been unkind to her again and again, and she was suddenly aware of her intense fury to the point where she was frightened of her feelings. We knelt beside her to share her tears and her despair. But as we prayed for the loving touch of Jesus, we began to sense a new mood. The room became more and more quiet. It seemed cold and bare, dark with something we did not understand.

Then our friend spoke in a tiny child's voice: "Mother, why don't you love me? Mother, why don't you *love* me?" Sobs shook her and, as we continued to hold her close, my eyes were wet, too. She was apparently experiencing the same sort of feelings I had had all too recently myself. Into the silence that followed her cry, one of the ladies spoke gently, asking Jesus to touch the moment when the little girl first experienced the helplessness and fear involved in her realization that her mother did not, indeed, love her. It was plain to see that a spot in the child's personality had been so hurt by her awareness of her mother's lack of love that it had remained retarded like a rosebud picked too soon.

We prayed for wholeness and Jesus' love, perfect understanding, normal development, and whatever else the child-in-our-adult-friend needed to become all it was possible to be. We described and visualized the presence of him who always healed whatever hurt was offered him, until finally the room became warm and the day became light with a new joy.

"What if I hadn't been angry with my husband?" she laughed as we all prepared to leave. Again I saw my own dull pencils. Her anger had been sharp and demanding, directing us to the heart of a serious problem. How often she must have fought down a surge of rage that she could not understand before her Savior took it and made her whole.

As it usually is with new insights, I had one chance after another to put my realization about the "pointing" nature of anger into practice. A man came and asked us to pray for his wife. Her problem, he explained, was that she would become so nervous and disagreeable whenever the family began to make plans to go on a trip that it almost put a stop to the expedition. She couldn't pack or prepare without surrendering to unmanageable tension.

"I am so angry with her that I have lost my own perspective," the man concluded. "I sin and I confess, and then immediately I sin again. What can I do?" Here was the anger again, only this time it was pointing not to just one, but to two things. We allowed him to sit in while we prayed for his wife. We asked the husband's anger to indicate whatever it was for which we needed to pray.

As we did so, we saw a mental picture of a little girl of perhaps two years of age being pulled out of a warm crib, hurriedly stuffed into a snowsuit and carried to a waiting car. It was dark. We saw the child awaken in fear, cry out, and be hushed. She reached for her comforting blanket and teddy bear, only to find them missing. We felt her terror and her sense of loss, and we experienced the tension and confusion of that moment for her. Her parents understood the reason for this hurried nighttime trip away from home, but the child did not. She had no way of knowing that her absence would be merely temporary, and the resulting fear that she had lost forever her safe, happy home had created a dent in her wholeness which was interfering with her happy marriage at age forty. Every time she planned a trip, her subconscious moved back to her fearful baby moment and her discomfort became anger.

As the husband sat in for his wife, we prayed that she could feel the loving presence of Jesus in every moment of the event of that first frightening move. After the prayer, we sat reviewing the episode. The husband knew of and could confirm that his wife had had such an experience. As we talked, the word "depression" came into my mind. Because it would not go away, I finally said it aloud. The man we prayed with seemed surprised.

"I was just now thinking," he said, "of the Depression. I was born in the worst year of the big Depression. I was the youngest of seven children, and I was always getting the message that I was 'one too many' in my family. In fact, I remember always worrying that we'd have to move because our house was too small and I was the 'extra' who made the house seem so small." He stopped, shoulders hunched.

We bowed our heads again in prayer. As we prayed, we realized that one of the reasons his wife's nervousness had made him so angry was because our friend had a deep hurt of his own which her behavior opened up. He didn't really know that nobody is ever "extra" in God's plan. He had never felt at a deep level that before the world was, God planned for each of us. Perhaps in the lives of overextended, tired parents, that baby had seemed too much of a burden, but to God, each person is equally desired and loved.

We prayed some more for our friend, asking Jesus to heal his hurts. As we did, we saw again that those who pray for the healing of long-ago anger at not being wanted must be sure in their own hearts that God did plan and want each person. Anyone who prays into such devastating rejection has before him a particularly important assignment: asking the Lord Jesus to show his great love and acceptance in a life that has never felt acceptable before. The freedom to feel such love is a gift that only God can give. But he does, over and over again.

The "happy ending" to the above story isn't all here yet. The wife did immediately recover from her nervousness at the prospect of a trip. The couple now travel together often. But his feeling of being only an unwanted extra is harder to throw away. Because it is a habit, and habits are sometimes slow to break, we have asked our friend to listen to his feelings and catch himself when he feels disproportionate anger—about anything. Nearly always as he takes hold of his surge of anger, he will see that it is pointing him toward a situation which has caused him to feel fearfully "unwanted." Then he can thank Jesus for healing that and find it disappearing as he claims the healing which he has had.

Many aspects of our history and our culture have caused us to fear and hide anger. Sometimes we have all done what I did: put it so far down into the depths of our subconscious that we do not recognize it exists at all. It takes patience to bring it out in the open and acknowledge it: patience and courage.

I have heard people in prayer meetings ask Jesus to take away their anger or change it immediately to joy. I know he does so under certain circumstances, for he is compassionate beyond measure when we are suffering. But as our lives grow and we choose and practice the deeper walk in his light, we find ourselves not begging him to magically change us so much as asking him to help us know ourselves and accept our characteristics. Once we have begun to do that, we can give our lives to him in greater depth and sincerity.

When God allows us to have the emotion of anger, he must have some good reason. My original picture of the pencils shows what we have done with one of the reasons. Anger aims a sharp, straight point toward a situation that needs attention. Jesus' anger aimed at the cleansing of the temple. It aimed at the chastisement of Pharisaic behavior, at hypocrisy and pride. It aimed at the relief of suffering and death. My anger can do the same. But before I am whole enough to go out and change the wrongs in the world, I need to let my anger tell me what is unfinished in the healing of my own inner hurts. I need to look at the point my anger is making for me, both in my own life and in the lives of those for whom I pray. For Jesus is there, knocking on the old closet door behind which I have hidden my unknown fear and fury. It is a real joy to ask him to heal the original fear that is still waiting to trigger a burst of anger. The anger has made a pathway from the inside to the outside, and Jesus will walk down that pathway anytime he is asked. He said, "I am the light of the world; anyone who follows me will not be walking in the dark; he will have the light of life" (Jn 8:12).

As I have been learning to help others permit their anger to point to its original inception, I am finding a great many new freedoms I had never conceived of before. When my husband has a burst of anger that his soup isn't salty enough or the onions aren't done to suit him, I can skip over the immediate tendency to defend my cooking, be angry back, or do whatever I would naturally do and, instead, say to him, "What are you *really* angry about?" If it comes out that somebody has treated him unfairly, which is what usually triggers his anger, I can remember that his mother died when he was nine and he still has vestiges of his child-fury (and fear and aloneness and confusion). I can laughingly reply, "Well, sure, that was not fair. But don't take it out on your soup. That's for you to enjoy." We can both then laugh and salt the soup together. When I find myself furious at some act of his, I can stop myself in mid-blood-pressure and find out how he triggered something that threatened me fifty or more years ago. Of course almost sixty years of habit has not gone out the window at once, but the tool is there for me to use, and I am enjoying the new freedom when I remember to use it.

Another vegetable the artesian well has been watering

since that day on the lake shore when I decided to give my five loaves and two fishes to the Lord Jesus is my new emotional reaction to God the Father. For a long time I joined many of my friends in thinking of God as a punishing Father who was watching and waiting for me to sin so he could jump on me. I watched both myself and others for evidence of sinful behavior. As I began to trace my anger back to its source and deliberately offer it to Jesus, I found that I was really free to see God as a *loving* Father. Just as I don't watch my own children every minute, hoping they'll be naughty so I can spank them, I found that neither does God. I began to search the Scriptures for evidences of his love, caring, forgiveness, patience, understanding, and long-suffering. Certainly he abhors sin. But he loves us beyond our largest expectations. He has made provision for our sinfulness. We often feel so guilty and so in need of punishment that we don't *want* to believe in a loving and forgiving God. We are afraid of any study or technique that might gloss over someone's sin, and consequently we miss many opportunities to spread the creative power of love in our own lives and those of others. As Jesus gave me the gift of taking the pressure off my anger, I felt a surge of the kind of creative power that God's love really can be. It heals; it flows; it makes new; it comforts; it forgives; it satisfies. When we experience it, we find ourselves no longer in need of self-inflicted wrath which is so intense we must identify it with God's.

In the Bible we have the message that Jesus did not want us to nurse our anger but to get it out in the open and deal with it before night arrives. I can just imagine the meaning of his words, "nurse anger." We dwell on it and think about it, replay it, relive it. We enjoy it. When Paul said, "Be angry but sin not," I wonder if he didn't mean that it is fine to experience the anger, but we must not play with it and tend it. Instead we need to look honestly at it and find out to what ground situation it is returning. Then, before retiring, we may retire the emotion for the good of our lives and those of others, and for the Glory of God.

Verses for Prayer

"Righteous in all that he does, Yahweh acts only out of love, standing close to all who invoke him, close to all who invoke Yahweh faithfully" (Ps 145:17–18).

"If you make my word your home you will indeed be my disciples; you will learn the truth and the truth will make you free" (Jn 8:31–32).

2
The Second Barley Loaf:
Unforgiveness

I am standing with a jewelry box in my hand. Inside, nestled in the black velvet lining, is a red stone. It has many facets; it glows royally against its elegant background. I keep it well hidden because, deep inside, I am terribly afraid that someone will take it away from me. Still, it is my treasure and once in a while, in the privacy of my bedroom, I enjoy taking it out and looking at it.

One day, in my enthusiasm for my stone, I forget to shut the door to my room. Before I realize what has happened, there is Someone with me looking over my shoulder at my red jewel. I try to hide it, but he continues to look. Finally he smiles.

"Would you like to trade that for a real diamond?" he asks. I look at him to see if he is serious. Obviously he means it, for he begins to unfold a purple cloth from around a breathtakingly beautiful stone. He turns it over into his hand and holds it in the sunshine. I gasp. He has offered me a trade which logically I should have no trouble accepting.

Somehow, though, I am reluctant to take him up on his lovely offer. I look at my red stone. It has been a favorite of mine since I was a tiny child. I remember with relish when I first received it. I relive all the times I have hidden in my closet, admiring it, turning it over and over, thinking of the moment when I first held it in my hands. I am fond of it; I am used to it. Will I enjoy the sparkling diamond as much as my old red stone—even if it is of far more real value? I debate a long time. Finally I ask timidly, "Is there any way I could keep this and have the diamond, too?"

"No, there's no way. You may have the diamond, but only if you willingly give me the red stone." He touches me with a tender smile, but he doesn't urge me. He has made his offer and I must decide.

It was at that point I realized what my second barley loaf

had to be. It was truly difficult to give up the many-faceted red stone of unforgiveness I'd held in my heart for most of my life—even to possess the pure sparkling diamond of purity instead. Of course I had "forgiven" in the obvious situations. But all the same, I had become comfortable with all the feelings that I had about unforgiveness. It was justified. I had really been damaged. The other persons never repented. Besides, the remembered hurts gave me excuses for self-pity and self-justification: I had a ready-made excuse for continued anger if I needed one in a hurry.

More important than the above facets of my red stone, though, was one which, like my anger, I didn't know existed: my hidden unforgivenesses. Those were the ones I wasn't aware of but which moved me to behavior of their own choosing. Much like the capped artesian well, my lack of forgiveness popped up in strange and seemingly unrelated places.

I wasn't the only one. I once tried to help a lady who had been for years "unfairly treated" by one of her in-laws. She came to tell me at great length how badly she had been misused, maligned, hurt. I spent a great many hours praying for her and finally offered some suggestions about a reconciliation for the two of them. The lady was incensed. She seemed surprised and offended that I expected her to want to change the existing relationship. In fact, she was so miffed that she didn't speak to me for several months. Finally I saw that while her bad experience with her in-law was an excuse to ask for sympathy, an excuse to talk about trouble, an excuse to feel put upon and mistreated, she had no desire to give it up. Red-faced, I backed away—but not without taking a quick peek at my own responses to see if I might be playing the same kind of game with myself that she was. Sure enough, I could see many similar responses in my own life.

There is no doubt about the importance of forgiveness in God's scheme of things. Jesus mentioned the necessity of settling unforgiveness between people even before going to the altar with sacrifices. It is as if keeping one's insides loaded with unhealed hurts fills the available space so none of the Holy Spirit of God can be there. My goal in life is to have more of him in every possible way. When I decided that barley cake number two was the unforgiveness loaf, I had no idea how much of my own insides were taken up with it. As the reservoir of anger began to diminish, though, the specific instances of unforgiveness stood out more clearly. It became easier to see where they lay and to define them.

I had a problem with a friend once. She told me she felt me clinging to her, needing her, being dependent. She scolded me for telling her how much I'd miss her when she took a trip. At first I was hurt and angry. I went back over every word I had ever said to her and chided myself for doing everything wrong. I blamed myself scathingly for the misunderstanding and was easily prey to the feeling, "I hate myself! Why am I so stupid?"

It was hard to do, but I pulled my eyes off my own inadequacies and put them on the Lord Jesus. I thought about him. I visualized his dealing with the situation, and finally I asked him, "Please, dear Lord, show me what I need to know about this matter so I will not be dragged into focusing on my own hurt feelings."

I sat in silence, waiting. Finally I saw myself as a small child dancing to my father's guitar playing. I experienced the fun of my movements and the sound of his guitar and his deep bass singing voice. Then my mother came out. She made fun of the guitar playing and of my uninhibited dancing. She teased us until daddy put away his guitar. A particularly precious moment of my early days was spoiled in the deepest places of my subconscious.

More pictures came, showing me how my poor mother's hurts caused her to need to spoil special moments for other people. I watched her hurt her siblings and her parents. Finally I got down on my knees and asked for a long pure flow of forgiveness to move over my emotions. I asked for a healing of mother's hurts which caused her to react as she did. I watched in my imagination as Jesus went to mother and gave her such a tender gift of love that she no longer felt deprived and resentful. After I did that, I watched him being present while Daddy played the guitar and I danced. He loved the music and dancing uncritically, and, in his company, so did mother. He repaired the whole episode for all of us and I experienced a real joy in family reunion.

"But, Lord," I said, "how does this relate to my friend's rejection?"

Again I received a picture. Other people came along who spoiled special moments in my life. Each time one of those spoilings took place, I became again the little girl dancing with her daddy. I became a child with a child's responses. I ceased to think and act as an adult. I tried to buy the favor of the person who had the power to ruin something in my life. I became dependent and clinging, fearful, and anything but a free Christian adult. Jesus showed me an unforgiveness in my past which was interfering with my friendships at the age of almost sixty.

After looking into the relationship with my friend, I found, indeed, the event that she had "spoiled" and the place in my life when I had reverted to the emotional reactions of a two year old. At that moment, my Lord Jesus stood offering me a choice. I could ask him to clean house with this present situation and let his forgiving love flow into my tightly closed insides, or I could hold onto my red stone some more. A new step toward wholeness became possible as soon as I saw my option. "Lord Jesus," I prayed, "here is my second barley loaf, small and very ugly. Will you take it and help feed the five thousand? And even though I am giving you my unforgiveness from the past, it will have to be *you* who puts the forgiving into my heart."

As he and I worked together to allow Jesus' healing love to move through me, I could feel all sorts of new happenings. I could forgive my mother in a new way and I could see that I had also held onto a long string of unforgiveness against my father for failing to stand up for himself and for me. Of course there were all those who had "spoiled" things for me who required the holy love quickly. One small incident pointed to a lot of others! Was my heart as hard as that one glimpse indicated?

Yes, I think that maybe it was. Anger is like water: flowing and moving and channeling itself here and there. It can be dammed up and formed into a great reservoir. But it can be drained away, too. There is a place for anger in God's creation. Unforgiveness, though, is hard like a rock. It sits unmoving and inflexible until it is dug up and heaved out. There is no place for it in God's plan at all. My picture of the red stone was more accurate than I first thought.

After I began to look closely at the hard redness, I saw that it did indeed have many facets. I found first the unforgiveness against the people who had, in fact, harmed me—occasionally by their intention, but most often because of their own hurts and needs. That was one facet, but it was the one I found easiest to handle. As I could see and understand the reasons for others' hurtful behavior, I could become compassionate and hence forgiving. I spent a good deal of time inviting Jesus' forgiving love to pour through the lives of different people who had damaged me in some way. I thought it was all done long before it really was, though, because as I eliminated the obvious unforgivings in my life, some less obvious ones stood out in the clear light of Jesus' presence. I had never really forgiven my father for passing on to me his big nose and his short stature. Obviously he didn't do that to hurt me—or out of need or for any of the reasons I had forgiven in his other behavior. It seemed a stupid, selfish, ugly spot in the process—so much so that I tried to bury it quickly in my depths and not hand it over to the Lord along with the rest of the barley loaf. It was as if he said, "Never mind how it looks to you. I want it. Give it to me."

Later I discovered that I was not alone in feeling unforgiving toward parents for unwanted physical and mental characteristics. Many of my friends, once I mentioned the problem, confessed to the same sorts of hang-ups. I guess we all felt that, in order to justify being forgiven, someone must have sinned. I don't think that is the case at all. If I have an ugly red stone with shining, sharp facets poking my insides, then I had better get rid of it. My need for forgiving is at the heart of the matter, not another person's need of being forgiven. Many of the people whom I asked the Lord to help me forgive never knew I had anything against them. Nor did they need to. If my father had been alive to hear it, it would have been the height of unkindness to list my feelings of unforgiveness to him and loftily tell him that he was at last forgiven. Most people don't meaningfully hurt anyone, least of all their children. Even if they have done so with malice and ugliness, the matter is better off between themselves and God. I have noticed, too, that what seems like deliberate meanness often turns out, with the passage of time, to have been some hurting soul's only available response to a situation impossible for him to manage any better.

After I finished off the forgiving of everyone I could think of who had caused me pain, I thought, again, that the decks were cleared. Not so! I turned the red stone a half-turn and found a shining facet I hadn't noticed before. It was my unforgiveness against myself. One day that side of the matter hit me full in the face. I love cats, and once my carelessness had caused the death of one of my favorites.

"Lord, please forgive me," I cried over and over each time I thought of that cat. Then I asked the cat to forgive me. Finally it was as if I heard the voice of my heavenly Father speaking. "I have forgiven you and the cat has forgiven you," he said. "It is you who must forgive you."

As I prayed for his forgiveness to fill me and allow me to forgive myself, I felt a release much bigger than the situation deserved. I wept and wept. Finally, out of the depths of my subconscious another episode emerged. When I was in college a boy and I decided to "help" a lonely girl who had never dated. We had no understanding of her terrible life, I know now, and we were selfish and childish and playing at doing "good." Later we found out that she had drunk poison and been found dead in her room. I had no way of knowing whether or not what the boy and I tried to accomplish for her had been responsible for her death, but I suddenly realized I had always assumed the whole episode was my fault. It had been too frightening to think about, so I had buried it. At last, my subconscious knew that forgiveness was a possibility and the whole incident surfaced. With more tears, I asked Jesus to go back into that nightmare incident and pour forth his love, his tenderness, his forgiveness. I asked him to touch the girl (for he is not locked into time and space as we are) and heal her hurts, to redeem the pain which had become unbearable to her, and to allow me to forgive the thoughtless idiot I had been at the time. He answered my prayer. Finally, all these years later, I can look at the situation and love the girl, the boy, and even myself.

Forgiving myself for all the "wrongs" I feel I have done is quite different from being convicted by the light of the Holy Spirit and asking God to forgive me—and accepting his gift through Jesus Christ. When I have asked for and accepted God's forgiveness, that is the end of the matter. He both forgives and forgets. He puts sin to rest. Vague uncomfortable feelings of guilt, sorrow, and even anger and fear, keep me linked to my past. Nowhere is there freedom, for I am forever carrying a load of rocks on my back. It takes a mammoth effort to hold out all those ugly things from my deepest inner places and ask Jesus to take them in his holy hands. Oftentimes when I have cleared out those aspects of my life and my personality for which I have never forgiven myself, I am free to see, maybe for the first time, real areas of sinfulness which I had never before identified. Those I can quickly confess and receive absolution.

"Now is it done, Lord? Have I given you every crumb of the second barley loaf?" What more could I possibly dredge up in the way of unforgiveness to offer the Lord? Well, I turned the red stone one more time and found a brand new unblemished facet which had sharp edges on every corner. It hurt just to hold it in my hand. It was my anger at God. Who dares to admit that he is angry at the holy God, the Creator of us all? Well, once I saw it, there was no way in the world for me to avoid admitting it. There were several instances in my life about which I felt that my Maker had given me a very bad deal. And not only that, I knew about other people by whom I felt he had done even worse. Some of his animals, too, I thought he hadn't taken proper care of, not to mention starving babies and earthquake areas and various other items in his less-than-perfect world. I had a whole list of grudges against my heavenly Father. "Lord, am I doomed to the depths of hell because I need to forgive you?" I think not, for in his own prayer, taught to us by Jesus, we find that as we forgive, we make way inside ourselves to accept his forgiveness. Again, it is not because God has sinned (which of course he couldn't possibly do) but because of the hard rock in my own heart that I need to make a conscious effort to "forgive God."

Before I could do it, I had to identify all that I might be holding against him. It was easy to deal with the items about which I could be specific. Still something vague hinted at its presence around the corners of my consciousness. One day Hannelore's cat gave me a clue about my hidden anger at God. Hannelore herself was presently to go be with her Lord permanently, and she was fully aware of her condition. She had made peace with everything but the practical matter, "What will become of Catsy?" Catsy was a calico alley cat with her own ideas about most everything. I said I'd take her, although I had a full contingent of cats already. I was somewhat prepared for my cats to jump on Catsy and let her know whose house ours really was, but I was not at all anticipating Catsy's soundly trouncing every animal in the house, including the dog. After she had handled that part of her move, I was relieved to see that everyone, including my long-suffering husband, was willing to have her live with us on her own terms.

Catsy herself refused to adjust. Her mind was made up: she was going to return to her former home. Although I did everything I could think of to help her find happiness in her new environment, she would have no part of my hospitality. She sat at the door and howled; she refused to play or purr or even eat. None of the goodies I offered would tempt her to accept a new home. It is difficult to explain abstractions to an alley-cat, but I tried.

"Catsy, your former home is gone. If I give you the freedom you want, you will probably starve when the snow comes. You do not understand what has happened, but I do. I am truly offering you what is best for you and I love you in spite of your ungrateful behavior. Please forgive me and adjust to what I have planned for you."

Catsy's answer was an unqualified "No!" and of course she eventually managed to slip away and be lost. I would gladly have given her appropriate freedom if she had been able to adjust to the environment I planned for her. Her little pussy-sized brain could not comprehend that I was not a cruel tyrant but a loving friend who had arranged for her best interests. As a result, she was probably not long of this world. Sometimes I'm not sure my brain is a whole lot better developed than Catsy's. I manage to hold God's plan for me against my infinitely loving and compassionate Friend instead of letting go of my unforgiving red stone and adjusting to the spot he has me in.

God will not go away in a snit if I finally confess my need for help in forgiving him for his handling of his world. I can tell him how I feel (which he knows already) and accept the healing love of his touch on my hardness. Even when I have for years been doing what the Old Testament calls "murmuring against the Lord," he can accept it and heal it.

Supposing, though, I don't want to forgive God. Maybe it is easier to blame him for my problems than to cope with what I might do if I were free of them. Perhaps, like the lady who had great unforgiveness for her relative, a large segment of my life would be disrupted if I were not blaming God for my troubles.

I know a woman who lost her mother at an early age. She is justifiably angrily unforgiving of God. I can visualize the lonely, hurt child listening to her neighbors saying, "God took her. Wasn't it a shame he removed their mother from all those poor little children?" What small child would trust such a God? Yet when prayer and forgiveness and loving God are mentioned, it comes out that the woman's whole family has used their anger at God to excuse a disdain for every aspect of the spiritual part of their nature for years. It must be that nobody ever showed them the tender, caring God who would love to give them comfort—and they have never elected to look for him or his way of life as a consequence. There is some of that in me, and as I will to forgive others, myself, and God, I begin to be aware of deep-seated unforgivenesses that are like the sharp edges of my treasured red stone. For me, though, awareness is the first step toward wholeness. When I am able to see the dent in my outline, I can ask Jesus to fill it out. And as he fills it out, new things begin to happen.

Verses for Prayer

"At the beginning God expressed himself. That personal expression, that word, was with God and was God, and he existed with God from the beginning. All creation took place through him, and none took place without him. In him appeared life, and this life was the light of mankind. The light still shines in the darkness, and the darkness has never put it out" (Jn 1:4–5).

"All day long I hope in you because of your goodness, Yahweh. Remember your kindness, Yahweh, your love, that you showed long ago. Do not remember the sins of my youth, but rather, with your love, remember me" (Ps 25:6–7).

The Miracle of Forgiveness

I discovered right away that there was a difference between a red stone and a diamond. The red stone lay heavy on my insides, but the diamond is light like a breath of holiness, sparkling and taking up no space at all. A new freedom came into my life when I finally managed to get all the crumbs of unforgiveness given to Jesus. "You shall know the truth and the truth will make you free," he said. And he also said, "*I* am the way, the truth and the light." He is the truth, and when I begin to know *him,* he makes me free. Freedom is like a hallway. After we take the first step into it, we begin to be aware of many lighted rooms to be explored. Salvation is a never-ending, exciting process.

The first miracle which came out of the Master's hands was a totally unexpected one. My relationship with God the Father changed. I had met the Lord Jesus in a personal way, but somehow I had never made real contact with my Creator, God the Father. I had him all mixed up with my earthly father, and I was holding a lot of grudges against them both. One by one those began to lose their hold on me as I handed them to Jesus.

I had thought for a long time that I didn't have to forgive my earthly father for anything. He was a quiet, innocuous man who would not hurt any living creature. He was gentle and affectionate. What could I need to forgive him for? It was my mother, the dominating, manipulative person in my life, whom I set about to forgive first. And, with God's help, I did. I began to understand her own pain and her needs, to see the reasons why she did what she did—and that she certainly did not intend any of the tremendous hurts she gave me. After a while I felt no lack of forgiveness for her and could appreciate the gifts I had received from her which would make my life what God wanted it to be. My head forgave her, and Jesus, who died for the sake of forgiveness of us all, put it into my heart. As mother stood lovingly forgiven, new and happy in my eyes, my father remained alone. I was not seeing him in the way I saw my mother. I prayed for insight and realized, as I said before, that I had many deep grudges against him, too.

Daddy was orphaned at age three. He was brought up by a much older unmarried sister who, I have heard, always called him "poor-little-Walter." Probably for years, as small children do, he thought that was his name. He grew up with a built-in response to life which was compatible with such a name, and until he died at eighty plus, he remained in his own heart a deprived little orphan. It was not possible for him to defend me against the pressure-to-conform which was being put on me by my mother. But I sorely needed a defender. So deep in my heart I held a relentless grudge against my father—and I didn't know it existed. Finally I saw it and, with the help of my Lord, I could forgive him. Nothing happened. There was still a hard hurting spot inside me, prodding my insides. I looked further.

My picture of God was based on my picture of my earthly father. In my subconscious I thought of God as one who, though loving enough on the surface, when the chips were down wouldn't *do* anything for me. I could never trust him to defend me, and in my helplessness I held a fury so intense that, when I finally saw it, it nearly blew me away with its strong desert blast. The problem was not one which God had caused. It was one which my inner life had adopted out of unforgiveness and anger.

"Lord Jesus," I prayed, "please help me to rearrange the facets of this ugly hardness inside of me and find the full measure of forgiving for me, my father, my ideas of God. Pour forgiveness over me like a bath in holy light."

It seems to me that when I receive a new insight so clear and intense as this one was, Jesus comes the most quickly and the most surely to help. In the four Gospels, he came at once and with total healing in his presence when people called him in deep need. The same thing happened to me. A warm flow of holiness poured over me like water, and when it was finished, I felt like a child after his bath. Immediately a picture came into my mind.

Imagine a man who is in the business of urban renewal—of rebuilding run-down sections of the city. He has charge of razing the old buildings and then preparing the locations for new structures. First he plans the destruction of the worst area, always, as he works, envisioning what is to come. For a time, in the course of each rebuilding project, he knows that the streets will be full of rubble. Everything will look more like chaos than progress. The builder knows what is to come, but a passerby would have no way of anticipating the end result.

Now suppose the man who is in charge of rebuilding his area of the city takes a Sunday afternoon stroll with his four year old child. The workmen are momentarily gone from the scene and all is quiet. The father holds tightly to the hand of his offspring, guiding the little feet through the rubble, around piles of debris, away from holes in the pavement. The course he plots through the mess is irregular, slow, careful. There is potential danger on every side. However the father, holding his little one's hand, goes steadily and firmly through the confusion until he comes out on the other side. His child is interested in everything he sees around him, but he has no fear, for he is willing to hold daddy's hand as they walk. It would never occur to him not to trust his father to guide him through. He is so busy looking at what is to be seen that he only half-listens to the description of the beauty to come which his father is giving him as they move along. Still, in the back of his mind, he is absorbing the attractions his father is describing as the eventual outcome of the chaos.

When I made the decision to ask for total forgiveness in the father-daughter relationship, I suddenly became the child in the above illustration. I took the hand of my Father and moved with a new kind of joy and fearlessness through all kinds of inner disarray, knowing that daddy had only caused the mess in the process of building something beautiful. Finally I fully understood why Jesus said that unless we become like little children we are not able to enter the kingdom. I noticed that he didn't say he wouldn't let us in. He said we wouldn't *be able* to enter. I took a new step into the kingdom when I finally became a trusting child to my heavenly Father.

It seems that nobody ever moves without the rest of God's community taking at least a small step along with him. People began to arrive to sit on my sofa and tell me about the hurting places in their own lives which I could immediately see were caused by lack of forgiveness. My own process was not completed (and I dare say it will never be until I meet Jesus face to face at my death) and I was a bit timid about telling a stranger about it. As he usually does, the Lord put me in a spot where I had no choice.

The young woman was pretty and talented, well dressed, unusually poised. I invited her in with pleasure. Before we were comfortably seated, she began her story.

"I'm in love with the greatest man," she said, "who is in love with me. He says I'm the light of his life and last night he asked me to marry him. I love him and everything's perfect but . . . " At that point she burst into a torrent of tears and folded into my arms like a child.

"It sounds like a fairy story with a happy ending. But you are not very happy. What do you think the problem is?" I asked her after she had spent the initial emotion. We sat for a while, she thinking and I praying for her thoughts. Finally we began to talk the matter out.

It appeared that her father had been a moody, unpredictable man who would sometimes come home happy and cheerful: a full-of-fun, loving, understanding father. And other times he would come home angry, petulant, impatient. The children learned to listen to the way he slammed the door in order to anticipate his moods. After a childhood of such behavior, my young friend was tired. Her subconscious was saying "A man is a man and they are all like daddy," because she had never lived in the company of another man, day to day. Marriage loomed in her still-childish eyes as "some more of the same" suspenseful behavior.

It was obvious that the first step must be to forgive daddy. We started there. We brought the subconscious responses out in the open and talked about them, allowing Jesus' love to flow through every misconception we discovered. "Daddy" was not the same man as the lover who had proposed. All men are *not* alike. She could forgive her father and "all men" but we were not quite done.

"I am going to ask God . . . " I started, smiling to myself at my own new-found awareness of a heavenly Father who would, indeed, *do* something. My guest stopped me, horror on her face.

"My first thought was terrible," she told me. "I thought, 'Well tonight he might not be in a good mood. I had better not ask him anything.' That's exactly the way I always used to think of my daddy when I needed to ask him something." She sat there in silence. I pulled out my Bible and we looked at a number of references to the predictable nature of God's behavior. She had never seen them because a pile of hardened unforgiveness had blinded her eyes to the truth about love. "Forgive us our trespasses as we forgive those who trespass against us," the Lord's Prayer says. Jesus knew what he was talking about. Until we are willing to give all the unforgiving in our hearts to him, there is no room for his holy love. A hard red stone takes up room because it is solid and will not move.

Later my young visitor went home with a new bounce in her step, a new love in her heart—and probably walked into a new diamond engagement ring, besides. I sat for a long time thinking of the needs I have left unmet because I never knew the active, moving God who is ready and waiting to *do* things. Psalm 37:5 says, "Commit your fate to Yahweh, trust in him and he will act." I began to say it over and over, changing the accent with each repetition.

COMMIT your fate ... Commit YOUR fate ... Commit your FATE ... TRUST in him ... trust IN him ... trust in HIM ... AND he will act ... and HE will act ... and he WILL act ... and he will ACT! Each version says a new truth about God the Father of all his children.

A little boy gave Jesus his five barley loaves and his two fishes: his entire lunch. The Master blessed it and broke it and distributed it to the multitudes: five thousand men, the Bible says, *not to mention* all the women and children. And there were twelve baskets of scraps left over. There was enough and to spare from the child's little brown bag. God is certainly able to do all sorts of "somethings" if anybody is willing to give his share.

One day I said to myself, "If there is one more crumb in the bottom of the sack, I'll dig it up and hand it over for the Lord's miracle." And yes, there surely did appear to be a little scrap left in the bottom. When my red stone of unforgiveness became the second barley cake for my Savior, a trace of dust must have lingered.

"Here is it, Lord, that last bit of unforgiveness I can find in my heart, and I don't like it much." I am like my father in disposition. I am unwilling to stand up for myself or anyone else. I prefer peace-at-any-price and am gentle when strength should be shown. Although I couldn't see myself, other people have indicated they were aware of my sweatshirt which said, "GO AHEAD, WALK ON ME!" I never liked that trace of temperament which I learned from my earthly daddy.

"Forgive those who have trespassed against us?" Yes, the last crumb was that I had to ask my Lord to help me forgive myself for being who I was: *me.* "Love your neighbor as yourself," Jesus said. I must forgive myself and love the way I am so I can finish the job of loving and forgiving my neighbor.

That tiny bit of barley bread, left in the bottom of the sack, had its own miracle, though. I find that God does not want me to disdain who I am nor what he has allowed to come into my life. He has loved me since I was "knitted together in my mother's womb" (Ps 139). He wants me the way I am, at least at the moment. All I need to do is finish the forgiving picture entirely—the picture of that *me* which he created for *his own glory* and see what miracle he will perform. I don't know yet. More than fifty years of practice not liking the person I am has formed a habit which only a continual flowing-through of his holy presence will finally erase. Forgive myself for being like my father? Well, all right, Lord. I am willing. What next?

The "what next?" became a new learning experience of the value of one of our oldest and most important sacraments: the Eucharist. I found that when I first offered my self-image to Jesus, nothing much happened. I was stuck. And we all know how terrifying being stuck can be. I knew that one more step must be necessary in this business of handing-it-to-the-Lord. But I couldn't seem to find it.

Since I belong to a church which offers the Eucharist only once a month, it was several days before I discovered what that one more step was to be. On the Sunday when we celebrated the Lord's supper, I had a healing experience of magnificent proportions. As I took the elements into myself, actually swallowing them by an act of my own will, I knew a new dimension of my Lord's love for me which freed me to forgive my own sin and ugliness through Jesus' death for the sin of us all. How did it work? I have no idea.

The mystery of the Eucharist is just that: a mystery. No matter what we pray and how intently we ask for the presence of Jesus in our hurting insides, I know now that we often find that something remains missing until we partake of the elements at the eucharistic table. At the moment when we put into a physical action the desire of our hearts for more of the healing presence of our Lord, something new and awesome happens. Swallowing down the reality of the bread and wine gives our insides a divine message: he is really *there* to heal and to reform and to love. When I gave my self-unforgiveness to Jesus at the altar, I felt his acceptance of it all over again and with a double measure of reality. Things were changed inside. I knew I was more free to live out the gift that my healing held.

Verses for Prayer

"Yahweh, make your ways known to me, teach me your paths. Set me in the way of your truth and teach me, for you are the God who saves me" (Ps 25:4–5).

"And when you stand in prayer, forgive whatever you have against anybody, so that your Father in heaven may forgive your failings too" (Mk 11:25).

3
THE THIRD BARLEY LOAF: MISCONCEPTIONS

"I have been driving around and driving around and I guess I'm just plain lost. I can't seem to find Kings City." The little old lady stood in the door of a small-town service station, obviously tired. The attendant offered her a chair.

"I started at Newton," she said, setting her purse on the floor and leaning back gratefully. "Then I went to Happyvale and Produce City, then to Goodner, Perfection, Laborton, Pleasantville, and then Wellington. But I can't seem to find Kings City. Do you think you can help me?"

The attendant nodded: "I think so. For one thing, those towns are not on the road to Kings City. You'll have to get on another highway. Look here at my map. It . . . "

The woman brushed his map aside: "No! This map is right. I inherited it from my parents and they got it from theirs. It can't possibly not go to Kings City."

"But, lady"—the attendant was exasperated—"the highway to Kings City is very different from your map. It goes through Grace and Hard Rock Flat . . . "

Again the customer interrupted: "Nothing doing. I know I never have to go through Hard Rock Flat to get to Kings City. My grandfather told me years ago that nobody has to pass through Hard Rock Flat if he doesn't want to. And I'm not going to. I'm not."

The attendant was becoming weary with the pointless conversation. He shrugged with obvious disgust: "Well, I don't care how you go, you know. All I can say is that if you want to arrive in Kings City, you'll have to take the highway that *goes* there. Maybe your grandfather did give you that map. I'm not saying he didn't. All the same, it is *not* the way to get where you're going."

The woman picked up her purse and stomped out the door. "I don't care what anybody says," she muttered angrily. I'm not going to go through Hard Rock Flat and I'm not using that foolish attendant's map, either!"

The young man stared after her as she drove away. He scratched his head in puzzlement. "What's the matter with her, anyhow?" he asked of nobody in particular. "If she wants to go someplace, why won't she get on the right highway to it? Some people just have a few missing gears upstairs, if you ask me!"

What were those towns again? Something about their names was touching a tender spot on my insides. Had I, too, been trying to find the King's City by going on the wrong highway? Thus I came to discover barley loaf number three quite by accident.

A friend had come over for prayer, and as we prayed, tears filled her eyes. "I'm always so *unhappy*," she wailed, covering her face with her hands.

Without thinking at all what I was saying, I answered her: "But you don't have to be happy. Who says you're supposed to?"

We looked at each other in surprise. Jesus didn't tell us we had to be happy, certainly. Paul didn't either. The Old Testament never said it. Our constitution says we all have the right to pursue happiness, but not a word is mentioned about our locating it. My friend dried her tears and we set about to find out why we were so bent on being happy. Before we had finished our hour together, we had discovered the next barley loaf: misconceptions. The old lady's map to Kings City was loaded with the wrong towns—not on the road to her destination at all.

Happyvale was the first one on the list. What was so bad about Happyvale? I began to look at the ingredients of my third barley loaf with some new discernment. Most parents want their children to be happy. Mine were no exception. In fact, as I look back on it, I realize that their passion to have me "happy" came across to me as an imperative: I *had* to be happy. Since I have never located the faucet to turn on for the happiness to pour out, the only alternative that came to mind was to pretend. I found that difficult too, for I, like my friend, had seldom felt it inside. The only way to make a success of projecting the "happy image," finally, was to fool myself—to make myself believe I was a genuinely happy person.

I am good at pretending. I set about to make myself believe I was exactly what I thought was expected of me: a happy ranch wife, mother, hostess, Sunday school teacher, cook, cub scout den mother, campfire girl guardian, seamstress, housekeeper, pianist, neighbor, and on-call chauffeur. I pretended with all my might. Finally, years later, I saw that I was not on the right highway, and probably most of the people who knew me were aware of my misdirection.

"Lord Jesus, please help me see and offer to you those wrong-highway maps that I have gotten from my parents and my teachers and my grandparents and have made up for myself." Finally I could see that all the play-acting was holding me not only aloof from people, but also apart from the Lord. If I allowed someone to come too close, he might see through the game—or more likely he would make me admit to myself that it *was* a game. Emotions are real, genuine parts of ourselves. Unhappiness is not sinful in itself any more than blue eyes or brown. It is merely a fact of our existence. Of course I have been granted the free choice of what to do with my unhappiness. I can kill, steal, destroy property, fight back at the source of my misery. Obviously out of the free choice comes a great deal of potential for sin. I didn't want to sin or be on the wrong road, using up time and energy "pursuing happiness" instead of pursuing a greater awareness and love for my Lord.

As I began to look at the state of happiness/unhappiness which was to be my gift to Jesus, I realized the worst aspect of the town of Happyvale was its preoccupation with its own condition. If one is busy checking his happiness-temperature all the time, he has no attention left for the Holy Trinity or his neighbor, either. He has only attention for his personal interior. The misconception that I must always be happy had to go immediately. It didn't leave as quickly and as easily as one might have expected. Almost daily for some time it was necessary to bundle the unhappiness and the guilt-at-not-being-as-I-should together and hand them to Jesus. But as with anger and unforgiveness, gradually and with great tenderness he changed the focus. It was as if he were saying to me, "You can be *my* emissary in every situation instead of thinking of your own inner climate."

Finally I was able to leave the town of Happyvale behind and back-track down my wrong highway to the next one. Its name was Produce City, and well named it was. Many of us get the message that we must be productive or we have no value. All of my family was achievement-conscious. "Faith without works is dead," they quoted, apparently of the opinion that enough works would overcome any real need for faith.

"That's very nice, but I'm sure you can do better next time," was the most obvious comment my family offered about whatever childish attempt I brought home from school. It became second nature to become a pressured person who made good grades, did well on examinations, won contests in music or art. The vague undercurrent of guilt whenever I was not "doing something useful" finally drove me into a non-stop life of being not only a "happy" individual but also a "successful" one. However, no amount of success in my endeavors ever filled an uncomfortable empty space of which I was periodically conscious. I knew somewhere inside that I was neither happy nor successful.

In order to give a barley loaf to the Master, the little boy had to take it out of whatever kind of lunch bag was the fashion of his time. If I were to follow his example and allow my seedy little contribution to become a miracle, it had to come out of hiding. When I took a good look at the success orientation, I was aware immediately that it was just like happiness as a focus for life: it was entirely self-centered. If I *had* to succeed, then my attention and my time and my energy were all directed toward my own success. There was no room for learning to love and serve Jesus for *his* glory. My own glory was in the way. "O Lord, this ingredient of today's loaf does not look very good to me. Mixed with the have-to-be-happy one of yesterday, are you sure you can do anything with it?"

Goodner was next, and even the sound of it filled me with shame. I had always tried so very hard to be "good." Although deep down I was angry at the domination of my mother, when the anger was given over to Jesus and out of the way of my vision, I saw that I might have been rebellious or creatively different instead of eternally concentrating on doing exactly what was expected of me. At some time, I guess, I decided that the way to win the elusive approval of the authority figures in my life was to be "good" enough. Just as I suspect the scribes and Pharisees did, I followed every law with fanatical care in order to achieve the feeling that I was an acceptable little girl. I wasn't doing exactly what was required of me because I loved my parents and wanted to please them. I was doing it because I was afraid that I would lose my security if I didn't.

This barley loaf's ingredients were all bitter. Looking honestly at my real reasons for goodness brought me to my knees in remorse. Checking the biblical picture of those who were good. ("You hypocrites," Jesus said to them—"you follow the rules but you don't recognize love when he is standing in your midst.") I can see that some meeting of holy love is involved: we follow the rules for their own sake until we meet the one by whom the rules were designed, and then we follow *him.* It was difficult to follow him out of Goodner when I had lived there all my life, but I was determined to do so.

My friends helped me with a plan for achieving freedom from the self-glorifying atmosphere of Goodner. We began looking through the Scriptures for every possible ingredient of God's love. We came to see that his love is always creative. It helps us grow—it requires that we grow. We will grow in his image, Paul says, until finally we see him face to face. To get out of the "good" habit, we need only to focus as entirely as is humanly possible on the image toward which we long to grow. Being good for its own sake, then, will finally cease being a goal.

One of the pre-conceived ideas that I needed to hand to Jesus, next, was "perfection." "If it's worth doing at all, it's worth doing right," was the motto of my mother's family. She was an excellent teacher and she had a habit of requiring that I do and redo everything I attempted until it was perfect. I was an only child; there was no one else to share the time and attention of a "get-it-exactly-right" mother with me, and the idea rubbed off on me as well. Now I have no quarrel at all with learning to avoid sloppy, careless workmanship. But when doing-it-perfectly becomes its own focus, it effectively turns one away from a beaming-in on God the Father, God the Son, and the Holy Spirit. I guess the reasons all those little towns weren't on the way to Kings City was that they all go around in circles and come back into themselves. Somewhere along the way I needed to have permission not to be perfect and not to care if I weren't.

Jesus himself said, "Do not call me 'good,' for only the Father is good" (Mk 10:18). Keeping my eyes on the goodness of God might relieve me of having to be good and happy and especially *perfect!*

Laborton was next, and it was a really hard town from which to escape. My third barley loaf had all manner of odd ingredients, not the least of which was that of *work.* Nobody in my family or my husband's family as far back as the Garden of Eden ever had a lazy bone in his body. If I were to lie down in the sunshine on a bright spring day, I was immediately caught up in guilt. If I took a nap instead of cleaning the house, the self-inflicted punishment was more than I could endure. I had a strong pre-conceived notion that it was necessary to work all the time.

Of course I know that Paul told us that those who work needn't count on eating. But if I ate as much as my inner pressures require me to work, I would be as big as an elephant. Somewhere inside was a lot of balance to be obtained. And as with all the other pre-conceptions of my third barley loaf, the focus was always on self. I worked because it won praise for me or made me feel valuable or brought in some other necessary reward. I did *not* work because I loved my Lord and wished to make his world a better place for all to inhabit.

I did not succeed in giving up my urge to work. When I offered it, along with the other ingredients of loaf number three, I did not become a non-producer nor stop working. What happened was that I could make my tasks love-gifts to the Lord. It is still hard for me to let up on the pressure and allow the Lord to give me my job-for-the-day. However, when I offered him the crumb of seasoning that was in the little cake, he took it and did his own kind of redemption. It no longer belongs to *me,* and my focus is free enough to leave Laborton and go on to Pleasantville.

One would expect Pleasantville to be a spot of beauty and rest. Instead, it turned out to be a place of sham and falsity. A pre-conceived idea that it was up to me to keep all aspects of the environment "pleasant" for everyone didn't fit very well with the picture of love that God gave us in his holy word. Jesus himself said that those who follow him needn't count on their lives being conflict-free. The deep inner peace which he promised is a far cry from the surface "pleasantness" which I was so determined to maintain.

I am a cowardly person by nature (plus, perhaps, by training). I have a hard time standing up and participating in any sort of conflict. "Peace at any price" has always been my motto. Following Jesus, though, one has to give up that motto, move out of Pleasantville, and find the world as it really is—which is full of dissension, strife, fury, and sometimes physical violence. The pleasant atmosphere I longed for all my life truly does not exist except in the land of make-believe.

Giving the crumb of pleasantness to Jesus along with the rest of my third barley loaf was as hard as all the others.

Each of the aspects of the imperfect map we have inherited from our grandfather is apparently as important to us as the rest. Growth is part of God's kingdom. He truly put into the very depths of our hearts the need to grow into his likeness. When I took his hand and started walking with him, I automatically committed myself to growth. Jesus did say, "Be perfect ... " If I am not mistaken, "perfect" involves wholeness, and it is our goal. No matter that we do not achieve it until after-this-earth—we are still required to move toward it all our lives. If I am spending my time and energy trying to maintain a placidly pleasant environment, I will be avoiding the growth-producing conflicts, the real confrontations which will cause me to develop. I still like a pleasant environment, free from the gratings of truth-against-evil. "Lord Jesus, take this ingredient of my pre-conceived ideas cake and do with it what you will."

Last, I retraced my path to Wellington. What could possibly be the matter with Wellington? Everyone wants to be well, and many of us feel that if we are not, it is a sign that we are not on the holy path. Jesus certainly did heal everyone who came to him in pain.

It took some time for me to sort out this last of my pre-conceived-notions barley loaf. Of course, our heavenly Father made us with the potential for maintaining health all the time. But he also allowed sin to enter the world and live among us, contaminating our original potential. If we are to choose between good and evil, evil must have been presented to us as a possible choice. We are continually besieged with all the opposites of health: ugliness, greed, gluttony, idolatry, to mention a few. Morton Kelsey calls these elements of our environment "psychic infection" and nobody is immune to them. When our defenses are down for some reason, just as with any other disease, we are prime candidates for such infection. Blaming myself because my body has responded to some form of ugliness and I do not feel well is another way of turning in on self, characteristic of all the other pre-conceived ideas I had.

Since we are made up of body, soul, and spirit, "illness" can have any one of the three source points. If my spiritual life is not in focus—if I have my eyes somewhere else besides on the Lord and his love—then my lack of health may be pinpointed in the spiritual realm. If I focus my eyes on the bodily sensations at the expense of turning back to Jesus' gift of himself for my wholeness, then I am again living on the Main Street of Wellington. Or if my emotional life is twisted, it may be emotions not held up to his light which are causing the discomfort. Most of us do all manner of things in an effort to find relief from pain. Often we do not do the one which would bring relief: listen carefully to what our Lord is telling us through our bodies.

Psychiatrists tell us that we maintain any kind of behavior as long as it has some sort of pay-off, either physically or emotionally. Whenever a person is ill, he does well to ask himself if, in some subtle way, he is receiving a benefit from it. Jesus asked the man at the pool if he wanted to be healed, and the man didn't answer. Perhaps he didn't know himself. If he were healed, he might have to adjust to a new and perhaps very difficult way of life. Jesus healed him all the same, and I am sure he gave the confused man the grace and strength to alter his lifestyle to fit. Sometimes I find myself in the same spot: I am not totally convinced that health is what I long for.

At the same time, I also have feelings of guilt when I am not well, so the conflict further adds to the discomfort. Truly, "well" is an enigmatic term. It demands that I must decide whether or not I will focus my life on my health or on the growth toward the Lord Jesus that is possible, no matter what else is happening. He would have me remember that my body is the "temple of the Holy Spirit" and not to be disdained. But nobody was ever told to worship the temple instead of the God of the temple. As with all the other ingredients of this particular barley loaf, the one of pre-conceived notions, I must get my eyes off the erroneous map and onto the Lord. When Jesus said, "Seek first the kingdom

... " he was giving us a criterion for judging all of our attitudes. If they take our attention away from him and put it *anywhere* else, they are not leading to Kings City.

Barley cake number three had a precise recipe; none of the elements seemed acceptable to me. "Lord, are you going to be able to make anything of this one?"

Verses for Prayer

"We know that by turning everything to their good God cooperates with all those who love him, with all those whom he has called according to his purpose. They are the ones he specially chose long ago and intended to become true images of his Son, so that his Son might be the eldest of many brothers" (Rom 8:28–29).

The Miracle of Grace

The map on the service station wall mentioned Grace and Hard Rock Flat. If they were on the way to Kings City, then perhaps I'd better see about them. I had willingly, and as completely as I could, handed my old map over to Jesus to make whatever miracle he wished. I no longer felt bound by the other towns, although some parts of me still remained a little homesick for them. Habits are hard to give up, no matter how willing we are. Probably the little boy who offered his lunch to the Lord became a bit hungry before the miracle was completed and the food was finally passed out to him.

As soon as I began to investigate Grace, my own miracle began to happen. As usual, other people came along who were caught up in the old hang-ups that I had newly discovered. And all of us, without exception, as we weeded out the true from the false—the play acting from the real world—began to experience a new, warm, personal relationship with Jesus. The more we sorted out and understood our real selves, we decided, the freer we were to know him and love him. And, conversely, the more we knew and loved him in a personal way, the more we were in awe of the majesty and holiness of the Trinity. God the Father, the Creator, the whole of the light of love, amazed us more. The Holy Spirit present in the world became more personal to us. It was as if Grace, the free gift of his love for all of mankind, as well as the love with which he created everything that exists, became more of a reality and less of an intellecutal concept. Even our efforts at

59

being the kind of witnesses for Jesus which we felt he wanted us to be changed. I noticed it clearly in my own dealings with people. The pressure to "tell about Jesus" diminished and I became less tense and more comfortable. It was more as if I were living in a beautiful house. A newcomer to town might arrive to ask house-repair advice from "someone who is familiar with the local merchants and repair services." I might answer his queries: "My husband, who built this house, knows the answers to your questions. Let's call him in and you can ask him what you need to do and how to do it. As a matter of fact, I expect he will do it for you if you want him to."

Instead of pressing the presence of Jesus onto him at once, I began to be more natural—and probably more convincing. If the person who came wanted help from the husband, he would ask, and if he didn't, he was free to say "No, thank you." Most likely, though, he'd be delighted to ask because he could see by looking at the house I lived in that my husband really *did* know his business. Witnessing is obviously done easily by the person who lives in the house the builder constructed. I found, though, that if I am to witness in such a manner, I must first marry the builder and find out what kind of house he can build. I must know him well enough to suggest even to strangers that he might help them, and to ask him myself if they were shy. After becoming more sure of Jesus' presence in my life, I found myself with fewer and fewer nagging doubts about the quality of his workmanship as well as his willingness to be of service. Grace, the free gift of a loving God, finally began to make sense to me.

Sometimes it's hard for us to accept grace. We feel unworthy. I know I did. I wasn't "doing enough," so I did not deserve to live in grace. Giving up the old, long list of preconceived ideas of what I must do and be gave me the key to an apartment of grace for the rest of my life. No wonder it's on the highway to Kings City.

The other miracle of the third barley loaf was my understanding of the town of Hard Rock Flat. My pre-conceived ideas, given to the Lord, changed into a different conception of difficulty. A whole list of "difficulties" disappeared! I had a great deal of trouble living up to all the pre-suppositions I had put upon myself: goodness and happiness and health, work, perfection. When those were out of the way, life was not so difficult. They had made their own set of problems. But, of course, life being what it is, there were still many problems and hurts. However, instead of finding it imperative to avoid those problems and hurts, I started noticing that they were steps on a path toward growth. The under-developed qualities in my nature were being strengthened by hard situations—most of which seemed, by Divine order, to focus around my weaknesses. I am not fond of confrontation. As soon as I gave my misconceptions to Jesus, instead of riding smoothly along on a super highway, I came to bumpies of a teeth-scattering intensity which I could only negotiate by some kind of confrontation. Confrontation was a whole new world to me. I had avoided it so carefully that I had to learn the very rudiments which many people practice all their lives. A child who is alone with much older parents, restricted in her social life and protected from normal childhood experiences, does not find out how to confront. I usually ran away, as a child. It was difficult to accept that my "problems" were the gift of the loving Mayor of Hard Rock Flat, who knew that if I were to grow into the image I so longed for, I would have to experience confrontation. Yet as I willed to remember the value of Hard Rock Flat on the trip to Kings City, I began to appreciate my pain.

In the town of Hard Rock Flat, all misconceptions fall by the wayside at the side of the reality of growing. Pretending to be brave and perfect, productive, happy, and good had kept me, for most of my years, from understanding and accepting the real *me*. Yes, I knew I was a coward. I dealt with it in many ways, trying to solve the problems of living in a society which was often frightening. In Hard Rock Flat, cowardliness was treated differently. Situation after situation arose which required that I hold onto my faith and "live dangerously." Being arbitrarily freed of the game of being what I was not, I had to take a good look at what I really was. At that point, I discovered the glorious presence of the one who already knew what I was all along. He not only required that I admit how far from my pre-conceived image I usually lived; he also gave me many new opportunities to deal with the real person he had created. I had a whole baggage car full of cowardliness about travel. It was hidden in its own boxes and passed off as something else. In Hard Rock Flat, I was forced to confront each frightening situation, hold tightly to the Lord, and move out onto the highways, waterways, and airways. There was no choice. I was afraid of loss, and in Hard Rock Flat I was forced to deal with the whole problem of security. I was afraid of helplessness, so of course in Hard Rock Flat I must learn that we are always helpless unless we are totally grounded in the Lord. In each of the new areas, I felt my own inadequacies melt into his strength. I do not have to be happy or good or wise or perfect. I do not have to struggle to produce. I have only to turn all of my needs over to Jesus, Savior of us all. That is not easy, but in Hard Rock Flat often it is the only choice.

"Turning it all over to Jesus," though, does not imply, as it might seem, that I immediately just sit and do nothing, waiting for him to act. As soon as I could feel my misconceptions truly slipping away into his holy hands, I noticed that my life became fuller than ever. Under *his* direction, I found my new existence producing more, working harder, being more fulfilling and satisfying (and happier, too).

Hard Rock Flat is a stumbling block to Christians and non-Christians alike. It would be nice to be able to say to non-believers, "If you will put your trust in Jesus, your troubles will all disappear. You will have no sickness, plenty of everything, and no worries whatever." Instead, what often happens is that life seems to become progressively more complicated. To outsiders, it might seem that deciding to live for Jesus Christ made everything worse. Those who have given themselves to their Savior know that with his presence comes a far-down solid inner peace which transcends every external circumstance, no matter what happens. It doesn't always show on the outside.

I believe that when we commit our lives to the Lord, he is truly in control of the outcome of every event which takes place thereafter. If the circumstances of our daily existences are fraught with problems, then each of those difficulties can be looked at as a learning experience aiming us toward our wholeness—and his holiness. That belief sounds lovely, vocalized; it is much more difficult to remember in the midst of reverses, humiliation, sickness, loss. Still, when discouragement threatens to have the upper hand in my inner world, I can restate, firmly, my faith that God can and *is* making "all things work for good to those who love him."

Determining to look for the gift which he is sending along with each of my problems is a good exercise in finding the growth potential in each painful situation. Jesus did not say that I could expect to be happy or comfortable, or to have my environment always pleasant. He did say that he would be with me to strengthen me and help me grow in his image. In the long run, I would rather have the latter. I would rather take my focus off my own feelings and put it on the person of Christ. Maybe if my feelings are too "rocky" I don't have any other choice. Hard Rock Flat is apparently the only town at the mouth of a deep canyon, and nobody can avoid passing through on the road to Kings City. Remembering that we have recently come through Grace and are well on the way to our chosen destination helps us all negotiate Hard Rock Flat.

Verses for Prayer

"In peace I lie down, and fall asleep at once, since you alone, Yahweh, make me rest secure" (Ps 4:7–8).

"I know that your rulings are righteous, Yahweh, that you make me suffer out of faithfulness. Now please let your love comfort me as you have promised your servant" (Ps 119:75–77).

4
THE FOURTH BARLEY LOAF:
PREJUDICE

A friend called to say that he was bringing me a new pet. I knew that the friend's mother cat had recently had kittens, so I felt sure that my new pet was to be a kitten. First I found a bed—a proper one for a kitten—and an old clock to keep it company until it became adjusted to my house. I bought a catnip mouse and a stack of cans of kitten food. I went to the pet store and bought a litter box, complete with a bag of cat litter. A double dish was next, marked "Kitty," with a space for water and one for food. "Maybe I'll need a flea collar," I thought, so, for future use, I made sure I had one, as well as vitamins and hair-ball preventative. Surely there was nothing I needed that I hadn't purchased. I waited impatiently for the friend to arrive with my kitten.

When he finally walked up the driveway with a bundle in his arms, I was a bit disturbed. The kitten must surely be huge! And it did not move, even under the blanket, the way kittens usually do. I ran to the door.

"Here is your new pet." My friend knelt on the floor and carefully loosened the folded blanket.

"What in the world!" I stared, unbelieving. Out of the wrapping stepped a small hooved animal with spotted coat and bright brown eyes. My friend laughed gleefully.

"I brought you a fawn," he said, stroking the animal.

"But I was expecting a kitten. I have everything bought for a kitten. What will I ever do with a fawn?"

"You'll love her. She needs a home and she'll be a nice pet for someone on a big ranch. And I never *told* you I was bringing a kitten. What made you think I was?"

I stood looking at the fawn and thinking over the mix-up. It was my own doing. He never *had* said "kitten." Well, never mind. I would figure out some way to adjust. My mistake was not irreparable.

The picture above (happily fictitious) is one of the ways

we come into many of our prejudices. When my friend came with the fawn, I could see immediately that I was suffering from a misconception: a pre-conceived idea of what to expect. If I could adapt my paraphernalia and my thinking to adjust to the fawn, there would be no further problem. I could take the "kitten" items back to the store and exchange them for whatever one needed to raise a deer.

On the other hand, if I were so determined in my decision to have my new pet be a kitten that I could not adapt to a fawn, I would quickly show signs of prejudice. I might demand that she use a litter box, eat cat food, and play with a catnip mouse—and when she refused (as she surely would) I might punish her unkindly. Perhaps in my anger, I might even have her destroyed for her "sinful" behavior. If so, I would be acting out of a prejudice which would dictate ugly, inappropriate actions on my part. We are prejudiced against people who do not look or talk or behave in the ways we have pre-determined they should. We have pre-judged them without knowing them or understanding them. We have allowed our opinions to interfere with the love that Jesus held out to us by giving his life.

When I catch myself saying, either aloud or silently, "I don't like fawns because they eat phlox," I need to check back to see whether or not I am really saying, "I didn't like a certain fawn because she was not a kitten and I have never trusted fawns since." There is a vast difference.

When I became aware of the nature of prejudice and the pervasiveness and ugliness of it, I knew what the fourth barley loaf had to be: prejudice. The rest hadn't been too tasty, but I felt more comfortable with this one. At first I thought it might be really easy, in fact, since I grew up in an environment which included individuals of every race and mixture of races imaginable. My parents worked at the Indian School, a boarding school where anyone might attend if he had as little as one-sixteenth Indian blood. Unless it was acquired by osmosis, I had no Indian blood, and so I attended public school. However, all of my play time was spent with boys and girls whose heritages were every possible combination of Oriental, Indian, White, Negro, and Mexican. None of us ever thought about the color of any of our skins. We shared toys, ideas, quarrels, plans to marry each other, and all the other incidentals children give each other in an unstructured environment. My only regret was that my life was much more restricted than theirs and they had lots of fun in which I was not allowed to participate. We all had different eating habits, different customs, often different clothes. Sometimes I envied my friends, but I thought, as I looked back on them, that I was surely at least unprejudiced.

Prejudice, though, has its own satanic method of finding a way inside. I discovered almost immediately, as I considered the fourth loaf to offer the Lord, that I was furiously prejudiced against anyone who was himself racially prejudiced. Because many of my friends were mixtures of races, I bristled almost to the explosion stage when someone showed racial prejudice. It took a time of real soul-searching to allow myself to admit racially prejudiced people into the kingdom of God. Instead of being non-prejudiced, I had merely transferred my emotions from one victim to another. For those who feel deep hatred toward other races are, in fact, usually people who have been hurt in some way and are shielding their hurts as best they can. Racial prejudice leaves a great deal of room for willful sin, but, like the color of our eyes, we are often not responsible for the beginnings of our prejudices.

I prayed for a woman once who was so fearful of dogs that she could not allow her children even to think of owning one. They begged and begged. Intellectually, their mother wanted them to have the experience of caring for a pet. She asked for prayer, saying, "I realize that I am prejudiced against dogs and even against dog owners. Still, my children so wish for a pet that I would like to recover from my feelings. Do you think the Lord would be bothered with such a matter?"

I reassured her that I believed the Lord, who knows about every sparrow's fall to the ground, would happily help her with the situation. We prayed for her until I received, by the power of the Holy Spirit, a mental picture of a child being badly frightened by a large snarling dog. I asked the Lord to heal the fear which had accompanied the experience and give her, in its place, a freedom from all her antagonistic feelings toward dogs. She did not remember such an event, but later her mother confirmed the picture and told about the experience which had occurred when the lady was a crawling infant. Of course, the child did not become fearful of dogs out of sinfulness or willing malice. The fright had left her emotions so hurt that whenever she saw a dog, she immediately put up defenses against him. Even the owners of dogs were suspect lest their pets reopen the original terror. Her wholeness with regard to love for all of God's creatures was severely interfered with.

This particular lady's prejudice dissolved quickly as we asked Jesus to be present in the frightened moment in her emotional memory and pour his loving light into it. The lady was willing to deny her fear-habit when she knew that Jesus had taken away her original pain, and her prejudice disappeared. Her children now own two dogs, a cat and five rabbits (perhaps more, by now).

Anything that frightens us, gives us pain, or disappoints us has the propensity for starting a lifetime prejudice. Even the well-meant warnings of others, stemming from their own experiences, can start the prejudice-wheels turning. The only way to clear out pre-judgments, apparently, is to find them and ask the Lord to replace them with positive responses. When I decided that barley loaf number four needed to be prejudice, to accompany the previous cake of pre-conceived ideas, I began to look seriously at those unexpected ones I might be carrying around with me. Learning to live with a fawn instead of a kitten required a whole new outlook on life.

Once I set out to make a scarecrow. I borrowed a worn

shirt and overalls from my father and a hat from my mother. I took a neighbor's cast-off gloves with holes in them. Last, in the trash, I found a much-used mop and a pair of floppy bedroom slippers. These I assembled on a broom handle by tying the legs of the overalls and filling the cavity with lawn clippings. It was a good scarecrow. It kept away robins and bluebirds, wrens, chickadees, and yellow warblers. The ravens, crows, and magpies flocked around it, investigating its every crook and wrinkle. A caterpillar made a nest in the mop and wasps used the lawn clippings for their summer dwelling place. It became so full of noisy or stinging creatures that I finally had to ask my father to remove it to eliminate them from my play yard. I think that my scarecrow was a good picture of most of our collections of prejudices. I had made most of mine out of the worn-out and discarded relics from my parents, my grandparents, my neighbors, and the back-yard trash can. After a while they collected so many odd and unpleasant stingers that I finally had to ask the heavenly Father to rid me of them.

I truly thought that my own prejudices were mostly the little wasps in the scarecrow. I asked my Father to set fire to the whole mess and get it out of my way, feeling that I could identify and renounce whatever was there without difficulty. When I had sorted out a small pile of family-related hangups and some obvious and not-so-serious little matters, I sat back smugly to wait for the miracle.

Instead, there stood the Lord Jesus pointing to my lunch sack and smiling sadly. He knew, but I had never before seen, the big prejudice which had poisoned my relationships for most of my life. I was prejudiced against men. When I realized the extent of it, and the ugliness, and the devilish way it had permeated every part of my existence, I was almost too shocked to move. It was hard to begin even to admit it, not to mention giving it to Jesus. However, he waited, hand outstretched, and finally I took the first step toward relinquishment. There were many disillusionments in my parents' past lives which had started the ugly plant of

71

man-hatred in the family. And its perpetration was every-where, subtly giving me the message that nobody ever likes or trusts a man. "He requires everything from the women in his life," the myth went, "and gives nothing but more and more trouble, more babies, worry, fatigue and finally death from overwork. He never thinks of the woman but only of himself." In a word, if a man is involved, the woman must beware. I, who thought I was reasonably unprejudiced, dis-covered one so big that almost my every activity was col-ored by it.

As I looked at what the man-prejudice had done in my life, I was horrified. It was not only God who had suffered from my out-of-focus. (I'm sure it saddened him, as all of our sins do.) But I saw with a shudder how my prejudice had robbed me. I had failed to listen to any male human being with the honesty and caring that was needed to hear the Lord speaking to me. I only half-heard my husband, a fine man who loved me in spite of my hang-ups; I partly tuned out the minister who was commissioned to speak to me the words of God; I neglected to let the Christian leaders, speakers, singers, radio announcers, and television person-alities get past a certain self-styled barrier. And so I missed a great many words-from-God which I am sure were there waiting for my attention.

Worst of all, I also kept a firm hand in the face of the Lord Jesus. He was and is and ever shall be a Man—God's Man among the human males of the world—and I, in spite of my personal meeting with him, still pushed him to a safe distance because he was. The fourth barley loaf was the big-gest and roughest one of all. For nothing else in my life had put the barrier between me and my Savior that the unlovely prejudice against men had succeeded in doing.

There was no area in my existence not affected by this particular prejudice. It seeped into my attitudes toward every phase of the environment, from politics to lipstick. When the Lord finally showed it to me, and I became aware of its extent, I felt as I had once long ago when my daughter dropped a bottle of bluing on the cement floor of the utility room. Although I mopped and mopped, cleaning what I thought was every square inch of the room, I still, for months afterward, kept finding splashes of blue in odd places. They were on bottles, on the window pane, on the mop board, on the broom handle. "Lord, help me give you this man-thing and let you make a miracle of it."

It was not long before I discovered, too, that other Christians are not free from prejudices, perhaps as dark as mine. We often not only sneer at, but carefully avoid, anyone who does not look at Jesus in the same way we do—and even more so at those who do not look at him at all. He told us to go out and make disciples of all men, to spread the good news, to love others. In following his commission, though, it is difficult not to allow ourselves to become prejudiced against those toward whom we are commanded to give the gift of the good news. A person is unloving when he is prejudiced. I may differ entirely with someone's point of view. I may even believe that it is an evil viewpoint, inspired by Satan. I may do whatever I can do to convince him that he should change it. But in the process, I must not allow prejudice to enter against another person. God loves and God judges. God convicts of sin. I am required only to accept and love. My job is to introduce the Savior who will take care of any needed revision of personality.

In order to keep my role in focus, I must refer back to the ugliness of my pre-judgment of men. For me, all men were suspect. For some the "suspect" are black or brown or fat or sickly or psychiatrists or preachers or rich or divorced or smokers or young or old or long-haired or unemployed. The end result of prejudice is equally self-limiting and equally unloving. I seldom really *know* another person. I don't see him with God's understanding and love him with God's love. If I did, I might be in a position to judge him with God's judgment. *Pre*-judge means judgment-without-yet-knowing. I must give this up forever.

God used a man to heal my male-prejudice. We had

gone to a Bible study and afterward were having a final prayer before leaving the hall. The man who became the instrument of my healing had come only to please his wife. He was not planning to pray aloud in a group. He said afterward that he felt impelled by a power greater than himself to lay his hand on my shoulder and ask simply, "Lord, please, whatever it is that Phoebe needs, give it to her. Amen."

I hardly knew the man and I paid little attention to his words. However, heat from his hand seemed to pour through me until even the soles of my feet burned. The group presently left the room, but I sat weeping like a small child for a damp half-hour. The next day I knew something new had happened to me. The fire of God's love for me had burned away my mixed-up attitudes toward men and left in their place a whole new attitude toward life.

It took some time and effort to root out the man-hating habit, but after a time I discovered that men are trustworthy, gentle, loving, needy, and longing for the love of the Lord in exactly the same way women are. Of course some men are neither loving nor trustworthy. Neither are some women. Likewise one can't trust every dog and cat and horse in his acquaintance, and sometimes even a dove-of-peace will fly overhead and drop something on the new hairdo. To harbor prejudice toward "men" as a classification is ridiculous. I feel sure that the same is true of every other prejudice in our lives, if we can look honestly at it.

Verses for Prayer

"Happy the merciful: they shall have mercy shown them" (Mt 5:7).

"You make judgments in a purely human way; I pass judgment on no one. But if I were to do so, my judgment would be true because I am not alone in this; the Father who sent me is with me" (Jn 8:15–16).

The Miracle of Trust

If I had destroyed the fawn because she wasn't a kitten, I would have missed a whole chapter of new experiences in the book of life. I knew almost nothing about raising deer and couldn't find much in the encyclopedia, so I learned from her what fawns do as they become adult deer. Because I was not bound by expecting kitten-behavior from her, it was possible to love her and teach her to love me.

The story of the fawn is partly made up. Once I fawn-sat for a friend for six weeks and I did learn a number of things about the forest babies. We sent her to the woods long before she was adult, however, so all I really know about fawns is that they love to nibble flowers, cry like a cross between a calf and a lamb, and are *difficult* to house-break. I also know that they are not a bit like kittens. What I know about given-away prejudices would make a larger pamphlet. For my miracle began almost at once after I was able to hand Jesus the prejudices I had held onto for most of my life.

For one thing, I began to trust and respect and, yes, even *like* men. I was safely past the flirtatious age, so many friendships grew and were rewarding for me and the gentlemen involved. Men began to share their feelings with me and ask for my advice and my prayers. The main asset, though, was a truly different emotional response to Jesus. Yes, I had already experienced a meeting with him which had changed my life immeasurably. However, there was much to be learned from him as a masculine example, as a Father and Brother and Lover that I could not even begin to (or even wish to) understand as long as I had a prejudice against men. The newness was a great joy to me. Immediately the Lord saw to it that I shared it with other women who had experienced similar warped relationships with the masculine.

Also, I found that there was a masculine side of myself which was not understood or developed. I saw that in disdaining the male element, I had also disdained a part of my own life. I began to study what psychiatrists have written about the composition of the human personality; I deliberately became conscious of the growth of my masculine attributes placed in me by my Father to supplement the feminine. Some of my timidity gave way to a more courageous approach to my world. I began to dream of boys and later men as my subconscious became free to accept the whole person I was destined to be. Over fifty years of living with the deep prejudice which I gave to Jesus left its mark. The habits of behavior had to be confronted. All the same, I began to see ways that I could help myself be free of them, and I set out to do my share in the process.

The most important and interesting result of the new prejudice-consciousness which I began to experience was that other people were soon making a path to my door to share their problems and troubles. Perhaps there is an aura or a vibration which others feel when one becomes less judgmental. Whatever it was, my new feelings must have communicated. People came to share the "awful" things they had done and the unmentionable events which had happened to them, asking, one and all, for a wholeness they had never had. Nothing they said ever seemed to move me from my own best-of-all newness: the awareness that my job was not to tell them how bad they were or what they needed to do to repent. My task was to lead them to know and desire the love of the Lord.

As I read the Gospels, I saw that Jesus' method of dealing with people was to heal and help and love and allow them to feel so special that they freely chose to change their sinful ways. I thought of Zacchaeus who joyfully offered to redo his entire way of life because he had felt himself loved by the Master. Jesus did not tell us, "Go out and judge the world." Instead, he said, "Go and preach the good news to the world." The "good news" is that God so *loved* the world that he freely gave his Son to save it. All at once a new and powerful freedom filled my life. It really was my job *only* to offer the glorious information of Jesus' presence to everyone who came to spill his or her troubles in my ear. The Holy Spirit would convict each one of his own need for repentance. I didn't even have to think about it.

If a person is dying of thirst, he will drink whatever water he comes across, whether or not it is full of algae and tadpoles. Without exception, those who came to share their sordid uglinesses were looking for a drink. They were dying of thirst for love, and, knowingly or not, were searching their hearts out for a drink of it. If nobody had ever given them a hint of its character, they might spend many aching years looking for it in all the "wrong" places: drugs, alcohol, illicit sex, money, power, appearance, possessions. My consuming desire came to be to hold out an introduction to Jesus Christ the Savior, to replace the water filled with impurities. "Look," I could finally say, "you have been hunting for something to fill your emptiness and you may have found a tiny taste of it in your unfortunate affair; but the real thing is so much better. Meet the real thing: Jesus."

After a while the "unfortunate affair," be it any of the fruitless searches we all sometimes make, will show up in its true colors because it has been touched by the Master. I find that, since my own prejudices have been given to Jesus, he comes more readily into the relationships I have with others. I am sure he was ready and willing at any point in time to come into every part of my life. But, like unforgiveness, those pre-judgments were solid, rock-like, hard-edged buffers against him. They might have felt to me like protection from the cruel world, but in reality they were dams against the love which my Lord wanted to flow through my life.

All of those who come to visit and have time of prayer are full of unseen and unacknowledged prejudices. Like me, their energies are drained off in believing and acting on their misconceptions. Much of my psychic energy was wasted defending myself against a phantom: the ugliness of the male. The men in my life had no intention of wronging me. My prejudice had not only sapped my energy; it had side-tracked the true goal of my existence: to know the Lord better. When I gave it to him and he so graciously healed it, I could help others lay theirs aside and find themselves revitalized with the holy love available.

Prejudices are usually hand-me-down protective devices from the past. They say, "It is safer to decide what is right or wrong for somebody else than to allow him to be something with which I can't cope." My fawn must use a cat box and curl around a catnip mouse because I don't know how to adapt to the natural behavior of a deer. To protect myself from her puzzling actions, I decree that she is a bad pet. If she further thwarts me by nibbling my nasturtiums, I may react with enough anger to damage her. As I began to understand the inception of prejudices, I could help those who came to talk of the nasturtium-nibbling actions of their associates by steering them into an awareness of the source of all human differences: the Lord. He alone leads us to the joy of freedom.

Even though I have willingly given my prejudices to Jesus, I find that they have left vestiges and shadows on my personality. The job is not done, once and for all. Even though a new freedom is present in every area of my life, I have to guard continually against the formation of new prejudices. They are lurking in the dark areas to jump on me unawares. I know that this barley loaf is the crummiest of them all, for no matter how many times I tip my sack, a new morsel falls out. Perhaps I need to use the Greek language for this particular situation. It has a tense called "optative" which is best defined as "in the process of happening." My fourth loaf is an optative loaf! But at least the Lord has it in his control. It is no longer mine. Amen.

One of the facets of prejudice which showed clearly after the bigger ones were out of the way was the one which mistrusted anybody who really and truly "changed." I had always prayed for change, expressed a longing for it, said I believe in it, but when an individual showed up on my horizon who was obviously different, I felt definite prejudice against him. I mistrusted and avoided him. It was all I could do to treat him with ordinary courtesy. Where this unhealthy prejudice came from is one of the family skeletons, but when I saw it in all its unlovely truth, I was horrified. The others were all identified and given to the Lord. Suddenly out of the woodwork popped this ugly goblin. Handing it to Jesus at once, with much embarrassment, I saw a lovely idea which has stood me in good stead, ever since. Belief is an intellectual process, to start with. One studies the facts and reads the arguments. He decides how different approaches fit into his own scheme of things, and then he decides to believe. With every other phase of life, when one has carefully—or even carelessly—made his decision, the fact or idea is incorporated into his life stance. I may read up on all the available historical data on George Washington, and decide that his presence as the person history shows him to be suits my belief system. At that point, I become a believer in George Washington. George, however, does nothing at all about my belief in him. The whole process has been on my side of the fence; and as far as I know, he sleeps as peacefully in his grave as ever.

Such is not the case with Jesus Christ. I search the Scriptures and the history books and ask people and research the person of Jesus and finally make my decision to believe in him. At that point he, not in the grave but alive in the universe, moves toward me. He comes to meet me as I go to meet him. No matter how far away I might be at any given moment, the instant I make a move toward him, he comes toward me. I may hold him back and make him wait, or the whole process may happen so fast that I do not realize it is a process at all. But he is committed to draw me to him by the very nature of God himself. Change is of God. We only turn to him and let him "do his thing." Now when I see someone who has been truly altered in his life-stance, I can remember that man can't, but *God can.* Not only that, but God is always using his influence to get me to exercise my free choice and turn to him so he can make me into the person the pattern of which resides inside my deepest self.

Verses for Prayer

"Now both of them were naked, the man and his wife, but they felt no shame in front of each other" (Gen 2:25).

"Whoever remains in me, with me in him, bears fruit in plenty; for cut off from me you can do nothing" (Jn 15:5).

5
THE FIFTH BARLEY LOAF:
HABITS

Narcissa took her shopping basket and began her trip to the grocery store. She walked out the door of her house and turned right. She had always done it just that way: turned right at the first crack in the sidewalk. She took three short steps and then a long one. She turned right again at the next corner, passed the first footbridge over the creek and walked to the next. On the other side of the creek she walked to the far right of the path until she came to the last block. The last block had a wide sidewalk and she carefully walked down the exact center of it. Finally she reached the grocery.

Inside, Narcissa walked to the shelves with quick steps. She filled her basket and hurried to the doughnut shop next door.

"You're late, Narcissa," Veronica said. "Where have you been?"

"I know I'm late. I've been shopping. Have you finished your doughnuts?"

"Yes, we're ready to leave. Shall we have one wrapped for you to take?"

"Yes, thank you."

There was a long moment of silence. Narcissa looked at her friends. For the first time, she noticed that there was someone else present. Veronica's sister was visiting from the big city. Narcissa realized that the sister was staring hard at her. She had seen this woman before and the woman made her uncomfortable. The stranger spoke gruffly.

"This is the third time I have been to the grocery store with Veronica. Each time it has been a year between visits. And each time I have heard the same—exactly the same—conversation repeated. Are you women a broken record or something? Narcissa, are you always late? Do you always have your doughnut wrapped to take with you?" She looked from one to the other of the ladies and they all stared back in confusion. Maybe she was right. Maybe the same thing always happened, year after year. Narcissa peered into her shopping basket. Sure enough she had bought the same items that had been in her basket the week before—and the week before, and perhaps the year before and the one before that. Perhaps there were different products. Maybe there were new ideas. The fact that she had never changed her grocery list suddenly overwhelmed Narcissa. She frowned angrily at Veronica's sister. It was not comfortable to have her habits questioned.

When Narcissa returned to the house with her full basket and her empty head, I realized what my last barley loaf must be made of. All the way along the process of turning my lunch to the Savior for his miraculous feedings, I had been half-consciously aware that even when my anger and my unforgiveness, my misconceptions and my prejudices were given to Jesus, I still had to contend with a vestige of each one. They were contained in the habits which had helped keep the uglinesses alive. In order for the whole miracle of my barley loaves to be effective, I must have some help in being relieved of them.

Living by habit is like walking in windowless halls. One turns when the halls turn, goes where they go, never sees out to where there might be new and wonderful possibilities. There is no freedom in habits. Even when old behavior has been wholly given away, the habits lock us into actions not noticeably different. There was no doubt I needed to offer my habits to the Master as my fifth barley cake.

Where did those habits come from? I wondered. Why did Narcissa always turn right at the third crack in the walk? Why did she take a short and a long step? The matter might bear some investigation.

"Narcissa, why do you turn right at the third crack in the path?"

Narcissa shrugged. She always had. She had never

wondered why. We asked her mother, who never forgot anything.

It seems that the first week after her mother began taking Narcissa to the store, holding her carefully by her little hand, someone had thrown out some rotting apples. They lay, gooshy and smelly, on the sidewalk; and shortly a line of ants, businesslike in their discovery of new goodies, began following the dirt-filled crack to the treasure. Day after day, little Narcissa was guided around the apples, away from the ants, down the sidewalk toward the grocery. Perhaps a small child might have investigated, explored, forgotten. But, held firmly by her mother's hand, she was guided consistently in the same path until her baby subconscious got the message: this is the *right* way to go—or perhaps the *only* way or even the *good* way to go.

A foolish tale? Maybe; but as I began a systematic investigation of my habits, I found several no more sensible. I have *never* sat on a bed. If there is no chair available, I will teeter on one foot to put on my socks, and I will carry my shoes to another room to tie them. Have I ever consciously decided that there is something eternally wicked about bed-sitting? Hardly. However, nobody else in my family ever sat on a bed either. I learned the habit from my earliest childhood. Probably somewhere in someone's past there was a bed with weak springs or a cheap mattress which would be damaged by being used for sitting. The mattresses and springs in my house would happily accommodate a small elephant. My lack of freedom was entirely inappropriate. I did not have to balance drunkenly on one foot when I might have perched quite comfortably on the edge of my bed.

To continue the saga of Narcissa: perhaps she and her mother walked to the first bridge and found it swaying a bit, as is usual for footbridges. Narcissa's mother had a dizzy feeling about swaying bridges and she avoided it. "Be careful, Narcissa. Don't fall. Look out, Narcissa. The bridge might dump you. Let's not go on that scary old bridge. There's a more solid one down the street."

Some girls would have slipped away and run across the bridge anyhow. However, Narcissa was timid herself and she listened to her mother's suggestion. Years and years later, she followed the same path past the footbridge and down the street to the other one, never realizing that she had allowed her mother's vague fears to form her habit.

Sometimes other more courageous Narcissas break away from mother and run across footbridges in spite of her. Interestingly enough, they often form a habit too: of doing *exactly* the opposite of what mother taught them. I had a friend once who ironed very awkwardly. I watched her one day and finally could stand it no longer: "Why, my friend, do you do that in the most inconvenient manner possible?"

She thought for a while and finally answered sheepishly: "Only because my mother, who was an excellent ironer, did it differently. I guess I felt that I must somehow rebel, so I started this silly method. I have ironed this way all my life: I am in the habit." We laughed together. However, seeing her habit and its foolishness, she was able to retrain her iron and ease her work considerably.

Of course not everyone is as timid as Narcissa. Brave Clarence came by one day, after Narcissa was older, and persuaded her to go with him to the grocery store. He strode happily along, whistling a jolly tune, afraid of nothing.

"Come on, Narcissa, have fun," he said. Narcissa followed him. But her cautious habits had not made her accustomed to the noisy friends who teased and galloped through the streets with Clarence, so when they began jumping out of doorways and shouting at her, she was terrified. She broke away from Clarence and ran home to her mother as fast as she could. Never again would she walk along either side of the street, thus giving the "boys" a chance to leap out at her unexpectedly.

Narcissa is more shy than many. Still, most of us have habits which arose out of the fear of some dreadful unknown which might suddenly appear in our faces from doorways in the street. My father was kicked by a mule once when he was small. As a result, he always gave any kind of equine creature a wide stern area. Maybe it was a sensible precaution. However, I have noticed that horsemen and horsewomen walk unconcerned around the rears of their horses without seeming to worry about being kicked. Perhaps my father's caution was not as much thought-out action as it was a habitual defense. Emotional defenses work the same way. If I, as a frightened bride, accidentally mentioned a subject which caused my new husband to lash out at me, I might refrain from bringing it up again. Long afterward, even though I became more comfortable with my status as a married woman, I might still avoid that subject because I had formed a habitual preventative against being hurt.

Other people's fears, passed on, cause a sympathetic reaction, and I have noticed that I am not at all immune to "catching" a habit along with a cold in the head. "Be careful! Be careful! Be careful!" is as bad as a sneeze to spread defensive habits.

Guilt forms habits, too. We avoid any situations which have ever caused us to feel guilty until, finally, the habit of avoidance is stronger than the desire to live more freely and with more trust in the Lord. My learning to assert myself is a good example of a habit born out of "guilty feelings." Asserting myself was "selfish" and it was "inconsiderate." After a while, I refused to assert myself, partly because I knew that I would immediately feel guilty if I did. The habit was viciously attached to previous inappropriate emotional responses. The barley loaf of prejudices was crumby, too, I decided.

After I gave the Lord my anger, I noticed that I was still reacting, often, as if I were still carrying that anger around inside me. I was continuing to bristle as if to defend myself, allowing my first response to a new situation to bring out the old reactions—even though in a short time I was able to see that the anger itself was gone. My *habitual* response had not changed. "How, Lord, do I give you my *first* response each time so that I will not begin the old, offensive process?"

As I held this most complicated gift out to the Lord, he seemed to be giving me two items: a big flashlight and a giant red eraser. As I took them questioningly, he appeared to be turning the light with frightening holy clarity on my inner world. Sure enough, he must have been saying, you can catch your reactions much more quickly. As I tried to keep the light in focus, I began to see when I was in reality not angry but was only acting initially as if I were going to be. At that point, I could stop and deliberately use the big red eraser to erase my habit so I could purposefully act out a new and more desirable response.

The Scripture quotation, "growing into his image," popped into my mind each time my first reaction was lighted with holy light—which kept me from being discouraged. In Colossians 3:10, Paul said, "And you have put on a new self which will progress toward true knowledge the more it is renewed in the image of its Creator." His use of the word *progress* gave me courage to continue to ask for Divine help. I was not made perfect in an instant when I started on the journey toward wholeness. I'm still *progressing* toward future condition.

One day I became aware that, like my prejudice about men, I had a habit which was tied like twisted string through all of my other responses. It was the habit of pessimism. For some reason, perhaps dating far back in the past, my whole family was pessimistic. For many years I thought nothing of anticipating the "something bad" that always seemed to be in the offing.

"If you want it, you'll sure not get it."

"If you have it, you'll lose it shortly."

"If you laugh too much in the daytime, you'll cry before night."

These were standard fare in our household. I am coming to discover that many people live in such an atmosphere. Yet pessimism is the direct opposite of all Christianity stands for. Certainly Jesus did tell us that we would have troubles, but he assured us that he would *overcome* the tribulations. He told us that we would eventually be with him in our Father's house. Even the thief, hanging on a cross as punishment for his anti-social behavior, was given holy hope. Pessimism denies his words, and, even more, it denies the whole of God's message through all the Bible.

God indicated through the holy word that He created us in love: that we have ultimate value and beauty. He offered us the gift of Jesus' death on the cross to redeem our straying from that pre-ordained purpose and restore us to his original position of pure hope. Pessimism denies the whole concept; it is ultimately a belief in the overwhelming strength of evil. Nothing from Genesis to Revelation gives a pessimistic impression. How, then, could I remain a pessimist after I had accepted the Lord Jesus into my heart? I didn't want to. However, the habit was so strong that, without my thinking about it, my first response to anything happening to me was automatically pessimistic. It was the habit itself with which I would have to do battle.

The war was not won easily. The hard part about dealing with the habit of a gloomy approach to life was that nobody bent on a pessimistic pathway can really see anyone but himself. Narcissa was so caught up in her habit of defense against the bad that *might* happen, the ugly she could see, the disappointment she fully expected to encounter, that she had no eyes for anyone else, even Jesus. Each day she had grown smaller as she followed her self-created rut in the path to the grocery store. Each day it took her a bit longer just to negotiate the bare essentials of her life. There was no fun; there were no shared doughnuts with friends. There was only nose-to-the-grindstone following of the windowless hallways of habit.

Perhaps Narcissa's story is a slight exaggeration. Or maybe, instead, it holds some seeds of truth. At any rate, I became determined to offer my pessimism, along with my other habits, to Jesus to do with as he willed. Almost as soon as I made my commitment, he found a companion to pessimism: worry. I saw that I had learned to spend a great deal of my time and energy worrying. If I couldn't think of something specific about which to fret, then I nursed a vague dread that was as ennervating as any specific could be. Worry is a side of pessimism which has its ugly fingers in many of the lives with whom I associate. To tell a person who worries, "Well, you'll just have to have faith," is as helpful as to tell him, "You'll just have to be a giraffe." Faith is not a commodity which can be purchased, borrowed, stolen, or dredged up just because the situation asks for it. "Give me faith, Lord," is sometimes answered by a fat red eraser with which we are to deliberately erase and redo our non-faith.

When I offered Jesus my bad habits and he took them and gave the flashlight and the eraser, it then became my job to use them. I found to my chagrin that I did not always want to be free of my "bad" habits. Sometimes they were crutches I depended on instead of my Father. Sometimes they had pay-offs in sympathy from my friends and in laziness about growing. The person-I-am and the habits-I-have-developed are not always the same. Sometimes I still catch myself accepting a non-productive habit instead of looking to see if I am growing in the image of my Lord. The habit-loaf is all set about with sticky crumbs, Lord. I'm sorry.

Verses for Prayer

"Yahweh called me before I was born, from my mother's womb he pronounced my name" (Is 49:1).

"So in the same way, none of you can be my disciples unless he gives up all his possessions" (Lk 14:33). (Habits, prejudices, hang-ups?)

Letting Go

There were small changes, yes—but the miracle I was expecting didn't happen. In fact, almost nothing identifiable happened. All the good results of the previous barley loaves were plain to see. Giving the Lord my habits seemed to have no results. Then I saw why. My whole life had been geared to unrealistic expectations.

Some of the expectations were pessimistic and some were optimistic (though not many), but most of them were not based on reality. I expected God to answer my prayers in the way *I* wanted them answered. I expected my family and friends to react to me in certain ways, mostly to meet my own needs. It was as if I were carrying a mask around for each person with whom I came in contact. "Here, put this on," I seemed to be saying. "Then you will be what I am expecting of you." It didn't work out that way. Suddenly I discovered that I had to take all masks off everyone—including my heavenly Father and also including myself. My biggest false expectations were of my own behavior, my thoughts, even my spiritual growth. If I were to give my habits to the Lord and receive the miracle from the gift, then I would have to let go of all expectations. It sounded impossible.

Bread has carbohydrates and vitamins, minerals, substance. It keeps us alive. But we need protein to grow. "Building blocks" are what my children's school textbooks called them, and they are essential. I looked again at the story of the loaves and fishes. Loaves are mentioned first, and loaves were what I had carefully offered my Lord. But the kid had fishes in his lunch as well. His mother knew that he was a growing child and needed his protein. So she packed him two little fish. Maybe I couldn't grow and help others to receive their own miracle of growth until I dug down in the sack and pulled out my own two fish to give him. Something about the last of the five loaves seemed to be definitely connected to the protein of my first little fish. I put all my expectations "on hold" on a shelf in the hall closet and pulled out the fish.

Verses for Prayer

"So now brace yourself for action" (Jer 1:17).

"There you see it: faith and deeds were working together; his faith became perfect by what he did" (Jas 2:22).

6
THE FIRST FISH:
WILLINGNESS

Supposing each of our lives is a river. Springs and artesian wells feed it. People draw water out of it for irrigating their produce and making beautiful lawns and flower gardens. They filter it and drink it, cook with it, bathe in it. Everything that has ever happened is either floating along in it or has sunk to the bottom. Or perhaps it has lodged against a snag on the bank and been retrieved by a child playing on the edge. The river is full of rocks, and because of them there are eddies and rapids. There are also calm, smooth places which reflect the sky and the trees overhead. The river moves inexorably toward the ocean, raging in wet weather and trickling in dry. Once in a while someone, or a group of someones, builds a dam on the river to cause more productivity and recreation. They must be careful as they build, though, to be sure that the intake and the outlet are available; else the dam will eventually burst. A Master has arranged the whole operation, but neither the one who watches on the bank nor the one who is trying to swim in the water really understands the entire design.

If our lives are rivers, we can choose what we are to do with them. We can be swept along, willy-nilly, swirling in the rapids and snagging on the tree roots along the banks. We can enjoy the periods of calm while fuming at the rocks and currents. We can be afraid of the debris floating with the movement of the water. We can hide our eyes from the decay we see collecting behind the biggest rocks. We can look at the whole process as ugly. We can try to stay in the eddies, floating on our backs with our eyes closed. We can enjoy the rapids and the thrills and scorn the diversion dams which draw life-giving water into the irrigation ditches. Our rivers are going to do what rivers do, no matter what response we choose to have to their activities.

The first of my two fishes—the protein building blocks

I needed to give my Master for his use—had to be my willingness. Without it nothing could move. Jesus is a Gentleman. He will not take what I do not want him to have. I could have shut my sack and kept the fishes for myself. So could the boy in the Gospel story. I decided that if the little lad could trust the Lord, whom he had only just met, to take his precious lunch, I had better dig into the bag and get out my willingness to give him, too. The boy did not know in the beginning that a miracle would happen when he handed over his food. I knew it. I had seen the miracle in person, as well as read about it many times. "Give and it shall be returned to you, pressed down and running over," are the words I grew up hearing. "All right, Lord, here is the fish of my willingness."

Easier said than done? Absolutely. It was as if I heard a clear voice echoing in my ears: "Willingness for what?" I couldn't just hand the Lord a vague spirit of willingness. I had to identify what I would be willing to do. Somehow, when I spoke them aloud to the voice I heard, the things I would agree to fell flat. Willing to sit and have it handed to me? Yes. But I have searched the Bible over and over for a Scripture passage which says, "Sit and it shall be handed to you." Jesus said, "Stand up," "Hold out your hand," "Take up your bed," "Move." "Accept." Even the "Be still and know that I am God" implies a certain active being-still. It is not easy and passive. Anyone who has ever waited in a spirit of anticipation, open to knowing the truth of God, is aware that work is implied. Willing to accept glory for my devotion and pliability? Yes, of course. But instead I have read the scriptural admonition to serve God for *his* glory.

The first willingness I could identify which rang any bells of truth was the willingness, in my river of life, to swim—not to float and coast, but to join my own creative energy with the movement of the river.

"Lord," I said, "I guess I must become willing to cooperate with what you are doing. The habits that have produced no miracle must be met head-on, accosted with effort of my own. You work, but I must help. I must accept the fact that my original anger, unforgiveness, pre-conceived ideas, and prejudices have been touched by you and healed, but the habits of behavior which I have developed over the years of my life to deal with those angers, unforgivenesses, pre-conceived notions and prejudices are my babies to tend hour by hour."

And so it turned out! Each time I prayed, "Show me, Lord," I was rewarded with the spotlighted awareness that a bad habit of response had taken over and crowded out the behavior that my new attitudes demanded. Each time I reacted to an event or a situation in my world with pessimism, the bright light flooded me. Then it was up to me to take the big holy eraser, eliminate the response, and try again. Over and over the pattern repeated itself until finally almost all of the negative, pessimistic responses were remodeled. I would say "all" except that so far I still manage to come up with one often enough to show me that a lifetime of habits doesn't give up as easily as I would like. Worry, one of many sides of pessimism, must be confronted almost daily.

It appears to be true, though, that if I come at pessimistic and worrisome habits head-on, knowing as I confront them that they have been defeated by the healing love of God, they fall much more easily than I first supposed they would. True to his word, the Lord Jesus is there in all power and glory to help me in my feeble confrontation. All I have to do is keep at my part of the creative operation: see them and say "no" to them as they appear.

What else did I then have to be willing to do? I must swim: practice and exercise. If the water was not to push me here and there, helplessly and futilely, I must put forth my energy, however weak.

The next willingness I found necessary to identify was the willingness to change. I found almost at once that saying one will change and being really willing to do so when the chips are down are quite different. My old ways of behaving are comfortable even when they are *not* comfortable. A paradox? Of course. I would sometimes rather be miserable in a way to which I have become accustomed than risk the newness required of me to give up my misery.

Women who are beaten and abused as children frequently marry men who beat and abuse them. They are used to it. They feel so unlovable and ugly inside that their deep selves are saying, "I need to be punished." The sweatshirt one wears when she feels such a need advertises it well—the mistreatment falls into place.

Emotional mistreatment is much the same. A constant barrage of what the youngsters aptly call "put-downs" forms an undetected groove which continues to drain in more of the same treatment. A person who was dominated as a child marries a dominating mate—and she is comfortable perhaps for years. Christian growth, however, finally requires some changes in the status quo. I had to give the Lord my willingness not only to change, but to grow into more of what God created me to be in the beginning. It is not always either easy or pleasant. The "growing pains" which make the twelve year old's legs ache in the night also hit the muscles of the soul as we stretch and gain in wholeness.

As I offered my own feeble willingness to grow and change, my first real bite of the flesh of protein, Jesus took it and offered, in exchange, his own impetus: his promise that we could call him "brother" and progress toward his image. "I will move, Lord Jesus, even if I would really prefer the easy way. For if you are going to make a miracle, you must have my fish as well as my bread."

The next bite of fish was almost immediately obvious. I must be willing to hurt. Christ himself suffered in order that we might be restored into a relationship with God. If I was to grow in his image, I found that there was a good deal of pain involved. It hurt me to confront: to cause someone else to be angry with me and perhaps say ugly things to me. It hurt me to be honest and to admit my feelings, frailties, needs, lack of perfection. It hurt me to see myself as self-

98

centered and to deliberately ask forgiveness for my own inadequacies.

Nancy, my prayer partner, is very different from me in many ways, and it hurt me to watch her learn *not* to confront, which she enjoys, but to be the one to give in to others. I had to choose between keeping the status quo or giving the Lord my willingness to ache from change, newness, growth. "Ouch, Lord. This willingness fish has a sharp bone somewhere inside."

After a while, I saw that each one of us has made a choice about every event, response, emotion, person which ever entered his life. Whether or not I was aware of having chosen, I still did make a decision. I am overwhelmed by the immensity of God's gift of choice. Even as a tiny infant, I could decide to a certain degree how I would approach life. One of the most amazing discoveries I made as I offered the Lord my willingness was that I did choose, and I must now be ready to accept responsibility for the choices. I must disown feelings of guilt because I had "made mistakes" or blame for failures and merely be open to the acceptance of the stances I had adopted.

Willingness was a small fish, perhaps, but one which was the key to a great deal of change in my life.

Verses for Prayer

"This is what I shall tell my heart, and so recover hope: the favors of Yahweh are not all past, his kindnesses are not exhausted; every morning they are renewed; great is his faithfulness. 'My portion is Yahweh' says my soul, 'and so I will hope in him' " (Lam 3:22–24).

"Every thought is our prisoner, captured to be brought into obedience to Christ" (1 Cor 10:6).

The Gift of the Spirit

It was the willingness to accept responsibility and to, by the same token, let go of "blame" that led me straight into the first miracle from the first fish. If I accept the decisions I have made for my life, then I must assume that other people are in the same God-given situation I am in, and I am free not to accept blame for their actions or their feelings. That bite of fish is a mouthful. It meant to me, as I saw the bright light of holy love shining on it by the riverside, that all of my actions are ultimately transactions between myself and Jesus. Even if they inadvertently touch other lives, they are filtered through my Lord. Therefore, each person's reactions to whatever happens are also between him and Jesus. I cannot "make" someone be unhappy, angry, frustrated. He allows what I did to put him in that frame of mind. *He* decides how he is to respond to me. Conversely, I decide how I am to respond to him. Holding onto the hand of the Lord, I began to try out this new (to me) approach to relationships.

A neighbor came to see me. She was angry because the water from our irrigation ditch ran over her lawn. The mistake was mine, as I am bad at damming even a ditch. I had a brand new choice. The miracle of the first fish had begun to happen.

"I am the one who made the mistake," I could say to her. "I tried to build a dam and I failed. Your lawn is wet because of me and I am truly sorry. Since I am unable to undo your unplanned-for irrigation, maybe we can find a value in it for you. What could you perhaps discover that is good in the situation? Is it all bad?"

At that point, having taken full responsibility for my error and deciding not to let her feelings dictate mine, I could offer the neighbor the choice of finding a gift or of staying angry. The reason I might be able to hold out the choice for her is that the Lord was beginning to free me of accepting blame for the way someone else chose to react to an unplanned event. I did not have to defend myself to her, which freed me to allow holy love to pour through the situation.

Willingness to give the Lord all of my habits and to work to learn new behaviors began to pay off with a new peace as well as another facet in relationship with *him*. True to his word, when I offered the fish, he took it and made a basketfull. All at once I thought of the list of the fruits of the Spirit in Galatians 5:22. To the degree I could see evidence of those in my life, I could be confident that anger, unforgiveness, pre-conceptions, prejudices, and habits were becoming positive instead of negative forces.

The first fruit is *love*. Obviously, as I could forgive others, more love for them could flow into the place where the hard rock of unforgiveness had been lying. As I forgave my earthly father and also God the Father, a new kind of Father-daughter relationship was possible. I began to long for more holy love. Finally I asked the Father to give me a double measure of it. I had been reading the story of Elisha and Elijah in which Elisha had asked for a double measure of Elijah's spirit. It seemed to me that in my world, extra love was needed more than anything else, and I wanted it to come as quickly as possible. Shortly after I asked, I was aware of such a flood of love pouring through me that I was both physically and emotionally torn, much as I would have been if I had contained an actual pipe through which more water was poured than the pipe could hold without rupturing. I wept and writhed, but after a bit I was aware of a difference. Without my own effort, others were receiving more love from me than before. I was fully alive to the fact that it was not *mine*, for my own feelings were usually not involved. It was *his*.

And as I experienced healing for both myself and my friends, I also experienced another dimension of his person.

The second fruit is *joy.* Oddly enough, when I became really willing to give up my habit of expecting happiness, the "joy of the Lord" came in to fill the cracks. As our wise minister once said, "Joy is the climate and happiness is the weather." When I was able to forget about the daily weather of "happiness," I could begin to enjoy the climate of "joy." Just as the "psychic infection" of gloom and negativism is a contagious disease, so joy is a contagious health. Innoculated against pessimism, one can become a vehicle for joy. A world which once looked drab changes into one full of surprises when one begins to view all of the events as directed by a loving Father (instead of an out-to-get-me Man?).

Peace is the next fruit of the Spirit. Real peace is not the calm caused by a big rock which stops the flow of water and makes an eddy of back-pressure full of debris—perhaps even a dead animal. It is, instead, the solid-though-moving foundation undergirding the whole fabric of life. All sorts of new peace which I might never know existed can come into my life as I begin seriously to turn my willingness to change and hurt over to Jesus. Being willing to accept pain if necessary frees one from defending so conscientiously against hurt.

I was always careful to prevent disappointment. In fact, the presence of the possibility of disappointing someone else or being disappointed myself hung heavily over me as far back as I can remember. It was a disciplinary measure and a censuring tool. It produced guilt. "I am disappointed in you" was one of the most demoralizing statements my ears could hear. One day, though, as I was carefully erasing a pessimistic response with God's big red eraser, I saw that disappointment is a close relative of pessimism—and no more holy or productive.

If God, my Abba-Father, really does have my life in his hands, and if he knows what is best for me even better than

I knew what was best for Catsy, then how can I assume that *I* know what was best. Perhaps I am playing God myself and thinking it would have been better if I had made all the plans. In short, he knew what I needed to do or avoid doing and he arranged the circumstances to fit. What I might think would have been a wonderful experience—and be suffering the sorrow of disappointment because I missed—must surely have been bad for me in some way I did not know. The Father prevented it and I need to be grateful. Well—what a surprise! "Father, thank you that I missed the concert and the wedding and was not the social success I expected to be. Thank you for protecting me from experiences harmful to my spiritual or emotional or even physical life. Thank you that I missed the party!"

At first I felt like a head-in-the-clouds unrealistic imbecile. Finally, though, I saw that, unrealistic or not, my health was better, I was happier, and there was a new peace somewhere inside. I could begin to say and truly mean, "If I'm supposed to be at the party, I'll get there." It is new and I'm not always ready to remember it, but someday I will experience a total freedom from the ugly, dark family of disappointment-pessimism-worry. Eventually we will all know that the pessimistic parts of our natures are no match for the love of Jesus.

Next comes the fruit of *patience.* I was overwhelmed by the space in my inner self for patience when anger moved out. An artesian well, burbling all over the landscape, takes up a great deal of space. The muddy ground may cover an acre if the well is really active. Piped to a nearby garden, the water leaves new areas for calm to develop.

With anger out of the way, understanding can begin to happen, allowing one to see others as hurting and needy instead of, impatiently, as obstinate or mean. As one sees others in such a light, he is able to stop making demands on them. He is able to refrain from asking them to fill *his* own needs. Nobody high-handedly insists that a paraplegic wait on his table. Yet, as we watch our own behavior with honest eyes, we often catch ourselves demanding emotional support from an emotional cripple or mature spiritual guidance from a spiritually under-developed individual. When we, of course, fail to receive what we have demanded, resentment has an easy access to our insides. Matthew 16:24 states: "Then Jesus said to his disciples, 'If anyone wants to come with me, he must forget himself, carry his cross, and follow me.'" True calm and patient real understanding come when we give our inner defenses away to Jesus and are able to forget ourselves.

Kindness and *goodness* are the next two fruits. I didn't know that the Lord took the five loaves and two fishes and made fruit of them until it began happening to me. Without the habit of inflicting my inner self with pressure to be happy and good, to accomplish my own work, and to make things pleasant, it became easier to be kind and gentle to others. When I won over the habit of judging, deciding, pushing, I found my sympathy and caring closer to the surface of my life river. As I discovered before, habits of pressure effectively keep away the kindness and tenderness of the Holy Spirit.

Goodness was a surprise, too. After all the years of trying to be good, I found that when I stopped trying for it on my own, there was soon room for the Lord God's goodness to begin to flow through me. Instead of thinking of myself as a "good little girl," I forgot to think about myself at all. It was at that point that I found God's activities happening through me without my effort to be "good." "Being good" and all the other self-centered "beings" can only go away when they are willingly given to Jesus, along with the habits they have formed. If the habits could be dealt with as quickly as the original problems, I might be a good deal farther along toward being "perfect" than I am at present.

Each habit and each bit of ugliness floating in the river of life that I could honestly and willingly offer to the Lord made more room for a deepening relationship with him. When I met him for the first time, it was as if I let him come into the living room of my house. Later I asked him into kitchen, then bedroom, bath, utility room. When I finally invited him into the furnace room and the little closets tucked up under the eaves, I began to know him as a faithful and loving Friend. He took the bits of saved-up hurt, the scraps of resentment, misunderstanding, loss, and fear, and put them together into many beautiful collages which have ended up helping others to begin to trust him and ask him for help with their own garbage. He turned out to be not only an awesome Creator of the universe, but also a kind and tender Pal. Each time I find and deal with a different aspect of the habit bug-a-boo, I know him in a new dimension.

Of course *faithfulness,* the seventh fruit, is obviously easier, the better our friendship becomes. When I am no longer caught up in pretending, in anger, in fear, in prejudices and unforgivenesses, there is more time and more energy to see ways to be faithful to my Friend. I can praise him more, rejoice with him, sorrow with him, work with him. He can be first in my mind instead of myself. It is beginning to happen—although, I suspect, only as a faint glimmering of what lies ahead. Often I lose it and sometimes I become discouraged. Then I look back to the days when I had not yet started offering my loaves and fishes, and I know that we (he and I together) are making progress. Yes, he is limited by his own gift to me of free choice. Still, I feel him not just waiting, but giving me a bit of a shove in the direction I have willingly chosen.

I didn't know that I was not a person of *gentleness* until after the day I offered my first fish to Jesus. He had accepted it, and I had been giving battle to the habits, choosing to grow, even when it hurt, and generally learning at my advanced age to swim in the river of life for some time when a friend said, "All of sudden you are so gentle. What has happened?"

"Was I not gentle before?" I asked, surprised.

"Oh my, no!"

"Oh!"

Apparently people who are deep in the life-consuming process of defending themselves against all manner of imagined hurts are not able to be gentle. Perhaps they must hold the world roughly away in order for it not to touch their tender spots, their childhood hurts, still stored somewhere in dark hideaways. In any case, when I accepted the healing love of Jesus' presence in my deep insides and allowed him to take my hurts and change them, I no longer needed to be rough. It was a shock and a surprise. I'm glad that I found it out after-the-fact.

Self-control is the last of the fruits of the Spirit mentioned by Paul. I used to pride myself on how well I controlled myself. Nobody ever knew how I felt, I thought. Perhaps not. I have had inklings, since, that many of my friends and my family members were more aware of my feelings than I was. Unacknowledged emotions often dictated my behavior and, although I thought I was controlling what I did, all kinds of contrary vibrations must have been coming from me. Children are particularly sensitive to one's true inner climate. Once when I thought I was perfectly hiding my anger, one of my little daughters astonished me by saying out of the blue, "Mommie, why are you mad?"

"I'm not mad. What makes you think I am?"

"Well," she ventured, cocking a diminutive gold eyebrow, "I know by the way you fold your tongue."

She was right. I was angry. But how she could tell how I "folded my tongue" when my mouth was carefully clamped shut, I'll never know. In any case, I was definitely controlling my anger—to let the pressure hurt my insides, ruin my joy, and disturb my children.

I am sure that the self-control mentioned in Scripture is something altogether different. In my own life, the only time my "self" is controlled is when I have acknowledged my true feelings and then willfully turned them over to Jesus to help me manage. When I can honestly identify whatever I have inside me, admit my lack of complete understanding, and most of all accept my inability to take care of it all myself, then my Savior seems to take over and the external behavior flows along with remarkably few hitches. My *self* is controlled by the one who created and knows it so I can be free and comfortable with the results. It is easier to see pitfalls and avoid them, to anticipate needs and fill them, and to put selfishness aside in order to operate with God's love. Jesus had no need to work at "controlling himself," since he and the Father are *one.* The more I become one with my Creator, the less I will have to exert my own control of myself. It's a glorious goal away from which I still remain a far piece, but at least I have seen the possibility!

Verses for Prayer

"There is nothing I cannot master with the help of the one who gives me strength" (Phil 4:13).

"Glory be to him who can keep you from falling and bring you safe to his glorious presence, innocent and happy" (Jude 24).

7
THE SECOND FISH:
IMAGINATION,
CREATIVITY, EXPERIENCE

Imagine a very old man who is so wise and at peace that he does not need worldly goods for his happiness. He lives in a small cave on the seashore, fishing for his food, and painting, for he is a wonderful artist. He has few clothes, little furniture, and is entirely happy with his life. His paintings are universally famous. He does not need to be conscious of his position in the eyes of the world. He has learned to live simply and love tenderly. Each living thing which comes into his life is treated with respect.

One day a little girl finds the old man painting on the sand dunes. He is not wearing fancy clothes, so the child decides he is a poor man—which doesn't matter to her, as she is poor, too. For a long time she watches, fascinated, as the old man mixes colors from natural materials to form beautiful designs on his canvas. The more she sees of this strange individual, the more the child is attracted to him. In her little-girl heart grows love, although she has never learned to identify her emotion. Out of her love comes a compelling desire to share something with the man.

The girl runs home and hunts through her meager treasures. She has very little to offer the painter, but what she has, she is willing to give. After a long period of careful consideration, she decides that her tiny pots of colored clay are the only possession worth taking to her friend, the artist. She packs them up carefully, wishing all the time that they were bigger and better. Finally, in a confusion of tenderness and embarrassment, she deposits her small package in the hands of the master.

"These are small, sir," she says timidly. "They are really very tiny and nothing of a great deal of value. But they are yours, sir, because, well . . . just because I want to give them to you." Her face red, she darts away, but not before the gentle old man has caught her and pulled her back.

"Thank you, dear child," he says softly. "I will always treasure what you have given me. To you it looks small. Do you know what you have handed me?"

Surprised, the lass shakes her head. They are nothing but little pots of colored clay—all she has above her most basic material needs. The old man smiles warmly.

"These little pots of colored clay," he says, fingering the objects in his hands, "are the three primary colors. Out of them, every color in the universe is made. With what you have brought, I can paint a beautiful sunset, full of a million hues and lights. I can paint every living thing, every dream, every sky-light of the far heavens. Are you surprised?"

The little girl is too amazed to speak. Her eyes glowing with strange new happiness, she stands on tiptoe and plants a kiss on the artist's cheek.

The second fish was made up, like the girl's gift, of three colors. I offered the first two pots to the Master Artist with my knees shaking because they seemed so small. Yet they were, I thought, all I had. They were my whole inner world: imagination and creativity. My Lord had made newness out of what had appeared to me to be utterly ugly. What, I wondered, would he do with my secret treasures?

When I was a child, my life, so entirely dominated by my mother, was drab most of the time. I was kept home from school as often as possible, prevented from playing with children as much as could be managed, fed bland foods, and generally most carefully and thoroughly protected from the outside world. It would be a surprise to my children, I'm sure, if I told them some of the pieces of information I did *not* know when I married. They had found out most of them by the time they were five. In any case, to compensate and perhaps keep my sanity, I developed a tremendously active imagination. Once I spent a whole year in bed with what was thought to be tuberculosis. It later turned out not to be true, but the year was nearly gone before I received a reprieve from the prison of bed and isolation. To make the hours bearable, I peopled my inner world with all sorts of interesting humans, creatures, colors, sounds. I loved words and spent a great deal of time playing in the dictionary, which I regarded as a *place*. I read all the books available, I spent time perusing the outsides of packages and cans, but, in the long run, I liked the dictionary best. I played with the lists of words I put down, making them do all manner of furtive changes in meaning, or making them rhyme, or making them agree with or contradict themselves. I turned them into colors (always brighter than the real world) and into music. I made up families of people, of animals, of flowers, of birds, even of stones and marbles. I made up "quilts" of the designs of words and sometimes even colored them on paper. I had several imaginary playmates as different as people could be. The best of all, though, was my game of imagining conversations in which I had access to some sort of wisdom which could offer hurting people or animals help and comfort.

Looking back at my child's imagination, in preparation for offering it to the Lord, I saw that it was most of my world. I lived there, slept there, and only came out when it was absolutely necessary. Could I truly offer it to Jesus, perchance to have him keep it and never give it back? It was hard to keep my eyes on the miracles he had performed with the five loaves and the first fish I had already given him, for offering my imagination was offering him my life.

When the day finally came that I could, like the little girl, take my gift to the Master, it turned out that I could not give it alone. I had also to hand him the others: creativity and experience. The imagination must surely be red in color. The yellow was my innate abilities, formed into me in the beginning, and the blue was my list of experiences. I was not aware that I had any abilities of consequence, and my experiences were—well, *blue*.

"Lord, and I thought this fish was so very special!"

It turned out, though, as matters often do with the Lord, that when his hands reach out to accept my gifts, they are immediately transformed into more, better, and more beautiful attributes than they appeared in the beginning. Whatever I gave him, he turned into what he wanted, and he began to use my offerings in ways I could never have dreamed.

The imagination, now in his possession, became a vehicle for healing and joy. In it, he came to show pictures of hurts from the past to be prayed for, cures taking place, changes to be worked on. He allowed himself to be more personal there than in the "outside world" and so strengthening my own awareness of him that I could confidently offer hope to suffering individuals. Because my imagination was at last *his* pot of color, I could trust him in his use of it and believe his living presence when I saw it. The scornful words, "It's just your imagination, it's not real," dissolved into laughter. "Of course it's imagination—not *just mine,* but *his.*"

The creativity, now also his instead of my own, could do whatever he wanted done. Limited only by time and space, I never could tell how it would work next. Never again "mine," all of the talents mapped out in my inner world could bubble up for use when my Lord wanted them.

The third little pot, though, was one I suppose that I felt I should disdain. It was the blue of experiences. I had always been reluctant to accept my experiences as being of any value. Most of them were, in my eyes, "negative." I felt that I was socially and emotionally deprived by the cotton box in which I was required to live. Pessimism, doubt, and frustration provided an aura around the memories of my experiences which caused me to be almost ashamed of what my life was made up of. Was I to offer a pot of murky blue to the Lord? As I asked the question, I remembered our tether ball.

My children had a tether ball which they enjoyed in summer and put away when the fall ushered in their wintertime activities. One year they tossed it in a corner of the basement and carelessly piled other summer equipment on top of it. Consequently when spring came along and they went to retrieve it, it was sadly misshapen. A camping gear box had pressed into one side and made an ugly three-cornered dent. The tent pole had printed a noticeable indentation, and the skate board caused a deep scar alongside.

"Mommy, Mommy, our tether ball is ruined," they cried, holding it up in dismay. Sure enough, it looked hopelessly unround.

"Never mind," I reassured them. "Daddy can blow it up again and it will be as good as new. Let him take it to the shop and fill it up. You'll see!"

As I remembered the sad-looking ball, I realized that I was as dented and misshapen as it was. Like its long cramped summer in the basement, I had endured being pressed out of shape by some of my experiences. Jesus gave the command, "Be perfect as your heavenly Father is perfect," and, as I said before, I'm sure that he also gave each of us our inner picture, printed deep inside, of the possible completion of our perfection. Some of my experiences have encouraged the potential, but some have caused the temporary indentation of my roundness. Like the tether ball, my wholeness is there in possibility, even when I look badly dented.

Every happening in our lives, practically from conception onward, makes its mark on our personalities. Pre-natal climates of fear and anger leave their dent in our wholeness, just as do early hurts. Lovely experiences, I'm sure, encourage the God-given potential existing in each of us. Whatever has happened to me, whatever I have experienced physically and emotionally and spiritually, in the past has had its own effect on my present. Perhaps giving my blue pot of paint to the Lord was one of the most important steps in the direction of a miracle.

When the old master accepted the youngster's three jars of paint, he explained to her that it took the three primaries to make all the colors of the wheel; and so it turned out to be with me. As the last fish in the little boy's lunch sack turned the miracle into reality and the little girl's three jars of colored clay turned the world into a glory of color, so my three-sided fish became its own blaze of happiness. All of my experiences fell into place in a way that nothing had ever made sense before.

It became evident to me that when I gave each of the five loaves to Jesus, he put more of himself into the empty space. As each of the five uglinesses was brought out into the open and willingly submitted to him, I was aware of a greater deepening of relationship with him. Like the long hall with open, lighted doorways, I began to see more possibilities, as yet unexplored but certainly present and inviting exploration. He has not owned my five loaves long enough for me to experience a total alteration of my personality. Still, inside in a deep place, I know I have changed. More changes are coming. I no longer doubt the alteration possible because of my creative Father.

But when I gave the fishes of willingness and imagination-creativity-experience to the Master, I got a surprise! I found that whatever I had always considered the most unpleasant and painful combinations turned out to contain my greatest gifts. Willingness and creativity, mixed with imagination, turned the ugliness into later beauty.

For example, for my sixth birthday, my father built me a rope swing. I loved it passionately, spending as much time in it as possible. One late summer day when I was going "up in the air so blue" the swing broke and dumped me on the ground with a thud. It knocked the breath out of me. Daddy carried me into the house and deposited me on the sofa where I alternately slept and vomited for a day or two. Nobody thought much about it, and in a short time I recovered and went back to my repaired swing. But what neither I nor anyone else knew was that I had broken my neck. I developed pain in the back of my neck. (I carefully refrained from telling anyone, lest I be put to bed and fussed over, which I hated.) The pain lasted until I was past fifty and the doctors discovered what had happened. At last inability to use my fingers drove me to a modern specialist who found the problem. Two surgical experiences later, I had a new, albeit somewhat inflexible, neck bone and a first-time freedom from pain.

For many years I thought that everyone had a sore neck and I accepted it as natural. I practiced the piano, often with gritted teeth from the pain, learned to sew, knit, draw, bicycle, and whatever else was allowed. Several months in succession in bed for other reasons did nothing good for the break or the hurting. Later, too, I began to resent the constant source of irritation. Perhaps because the Lord was working in the situation before I knew it, I made a conscious decision: the ache in my neck would *not* be front and center in my life. Whatever else I did, I would never let myself focus on it. It was a wise decision. I learned from my experience that one does not have to allow a chronically painful condition to dominate his life. He has the choice to shift it to a back burner and do whatever he needs to do in spite of it. Unlike debilitating pain, which has its own set of rules, the chronic misery in my life could be sidetracked by the Lord's use of my determination, imagination, and creativity.

As I look back, I see that out of the persistence of pain and the domination of my mother came the gift which I, at this point, treasure with a new-found awe: I know that *I can choose my focus.* Those situations existed and I could not change them. However, nobody could require me to be in bondage to them. By some miracle, I elected to put that precious focus on the Lord Jesus; and he, unlike George Washington, came to meet me. I also learned from the years of hurting that I could keep other kinds of discomfort out of the prime-time center of my life, too. Hurts hit me, but, like a spoonful of mush, I squished out around them and went on operating. My active imagination and my natural creativity given to me by the original Creator moved together with my experiences to produce "the gift."

Apparently it takes all of our separate parts to bring into being God's plan for us. Although I disdained my experiences, treasured my imagination, and denied my creativity,

God looked at the matter differently. No matter what happened to me (or, to my original way of looking at it, what *failed* to happen to me) it was part of a scheme for letting me participate in his bigger plan. Creativity, in his eyes, must mean participating, friend with Friend, in a program so big that I cannot comprehend it at all.

Offering up my past experiences into Jesus' holy hands gave me a new understanding of redemption. He died on the cross to redeem the world from the death brought about by sin. However, it didn't happen once only. The child's loaves and fishes are redeemed daily in our private lives.

I once visited a city which had an interesting plan. Once a week the newspaper published a series of "double coupons." If one took a double coupon, added the coupon he already had for any given item, and took them to the checker with his grocery purchase, the ensuing savings was noticeably money-in-the-pocket. Still, the coupons didn't work unless one took them to the grocery store and offered them up. Being hungry, I couldn't just eat the coupons and my dollar bill. I had to trade them in for a box of cereal or a bag of rice. Jesus' gift of redemption works the same way. I can try to live my life munching my past hurts, difficulties, losses—even my truimphs and joys—but there won't be ease for my pains and needs. When I take everything to him, who has provided me with a constant "double coupon," and hand them over, the miracles begin. My experiences turn into blessings, my imagination becomes a vessel for him to use, and my creative talents begin to bloom. I start to write and lecture, offer listening and love to others, make beautiful objects for everyone's enjoyment, and create in many ways I have never before known were possible. Those are his gifts: the gifts of redemption. Taken up and touched by Jesus, the child's five loaves and two fishes turned into a never-ending miracle, as alive and vibrant now as it was two thousand years ago. Not only did they change into glory once, but the glory grows and multiplies as time goes on. There are millions more people on earth today than there were when Jesus walked the shores of the Sea of Galilee. Each one is a potential miracle resulting from "Double Coupon Day." What I have experienced so far is nothing beside the potential for the future—until the day finally arrives when the words "Thy kingdom come" which we pray daily become his miraculous reality.

There were many hurts in my life; there are many hurts in everyone else's. Jesus never told us that we would be free from tribulations. As I listen to people in pain tell me of their grief, I can truly offer them the assurance that no matter what has happened—the deprivation, the ugliness, the illness, the loss—Jesus' miracle is that he offers us the total redemption of those experiences. The worse the hurt, the bigger the gift. Can we truly look at life with that sort of hope? First I had to offer up my anger, my unforgiveness, my bad habits and pre-conceptions, my prejudices. I had to become willing to *accept* having my offering redeemed into a gift. Everyone else is the same. We have to decide to be free of soaking in the soup of misery, to accept the miracle which is handed to us. The boy in the Gospels did not give Jesus his lunch and then run home as fast as he could go. He had to stick around and see the unbelievable which was taking place. So do I. First I offer what I have to the Lord and then I have to stay in the game, watching to see what occurs next. Maybe I won't see a thing for days—or perhaps months. Still, my eyes had better be open to find out what the Master has in mind. Wholeness is a big goal. It takes time. Each little dent has to be filled from inside with the Holy Spirit, like my children's tether ball being blown up. My ball had been scrunched in the bottom of the closet for a long time. When I began to allow the Spirit to exchange the wrinkles and the hurting ridges for freedom and the presence of Jesus, I was astonished at the changes. Nobody is too badly damaged to offer his five loaves and his two fishes to Jesus to find out what miracle he will provide.

Verses for Prayer

"Those who went sowing in tears now sing as they reap. They went away weeping, carrying the seed; they came back, singing, carrying their sheaves" (Ps 126:5-6).

"Jesus said, 'Well, then, every scribe who becomes a disciple of the kingdom of heaven is like a householder who brings out from his storeroom things both old and new' " (Mt 13:52).

The Gift of Jesus

In many people's minds, the use of imagination, of pictures, of visualizing, is suspect. We are taught to "keep in touch with reality" and not to fantasize. We are scornfully informed, "Now that's just your imagination working overtime." We are reminded that the Bible warns about "vain imaginations" along with other tools of the occult. So we become defensive about the sort of pictures I have used all through the pages of this volume. My pictures and parables and stories are not lonely, esoteric gifts. The Lord gives them to me—and to you and to you and even to *you*—as a result of deep prayer and communication with him. They are a type of gift which he gives as I learn to know him. The Greek word for "know" used in the statement of Jesus "You shall know the truth and the truth will make you free" is the same word used in Matthew to describe the most intimate union: sexual relations. (Joseph did not "know" Mary until after her Baby was born.) Prayer for a close personal knowledge of our Lord Jesus goes on and on. By practicing his presence, as Brother Lawrence did centuries ago, we become familiar with him and find that his stories and pictures and parables are everywhere. He is speaking to us all the time, in our imaginations as well as our intellects.

When we wish to come closer to Jesus, to *know* him better, one of the ways we can begin is to open our Bibles to one of the situations described and read it with our imaginations wide open. We can visualize the places and the circumstances, the odors, the colors, the feel of the air, the people. Then we can invite Jesus to come in just as he did

121

during his physical time on earth. We can trust that it is he who comes and not someone else because he assured us that if a child asks his father for a fish, he will not receive a scorpion. When we ask Jesus for his holy presence, he is powerful and faithful enough not to send a demon.

As we become used to the practice of being open to the gifts that the Holy Spirit offers, we find that our visualizations are not artificial manipulations or deliberate do-it-yourself pictures of Jesus. Instead they provide the framework for us to watch and see how he will enrich our understandings of whatever matters are important to us. If we are studying a difficult Scripture passage, he may give us a picture, a word, a gesture, or even a joke that opens up its meaning. If we are dealing with pain from our past, we may watch and perhaps participate with him as he heals. His methods differ with the circumstances. The test for anything is in its fruit. If the Lord touches my inner world and the result is a new and deeper love for him, more worship, more praise, more inner peace, love for my neighbors, forgiveness, patience, then I can know I have seen him working. Even if some of his activity reveals my sin and error (which often happens), my life is enriched by the renewed awareness that Jesus' death on the cross was the "balm of Gilead" which was for my healing through forgiveness. I may be alone or with friends when I sit down with my Bible and begin to "look" at a setting and its activity. I may be sad or glad, tired or elated. But I am always rewarded whatever my Lord has to offer. Sitting quietly, like Mary, at his feet, I look with inner eyes to see what he will do next.

We all need to continue searching the Bible for more information about Jesus; we need to let its words speak to us continually. We also need to let him speak through Scripture with more than words. He conveys his presence and his message through pictures and parables, the words of others, music, poetry, nature, hardship, loss, grief and the magnificence of his glory. We must not limit his voice nor deny his methods.

One day I was asked to make a talk for a "Day of Spiritual Renewal." I jotted down a few notes and put them in my left skirt pocket. When I arrived at the meeting, I reached by mistake into my right pocket. I pulled out my grocery list. On it was written

bread
cereal
meat
light bulbs
girdle
earrings
coffee
aspirin

"Renewal," the master of ceremonies said. My shelves and drawers had empty places in them. I had needs which I was taking to the city for filling. Perhaps the speech notes and the shopping list weren't so different from each other, after all.

Bread and cereal are basic foodstuffs of life. I had been giving the loaves of my inner ugliness to the Lord and receiving in return his miracles. If I were to acknowledge the deepest hunger inside of me, it would be for the bread of holy love that Jesus gives us in exchange for the crumbs of our own willingness. Meat is the protein of growth. I had given him two tiny bits of fish for his blessing, but I was longing for the hearty red meat of his movement in my life: of his growth in me and my growth in him.

When the light bulbs are burned out, the house is dark. The lamps will not fill it again with light until something new has been installed. I am longing for the light of his wisdom and his inspiration to let me see. I need new illumination in order to work and move and grow.

A girdle keeps me contained, in good shape, comfortable. Besides, it holds my stockings up. Jesus' love in my life surrounds me, smooths my contours, holds me together.

Nothing will wrinkle and slip on the outside if my inner shape is well maintained.

Having a little decoration and fun in my life doesn't spoil it; it enhances it. A bit of loving adornment given me by the Father who made me and loves me puts spice into my everyday world and laughter, too. I can afford to be a bit frivolous with the omnipresence of love. I can even decorate my ears!

Sometimes we feel a need to be artificially stimulated, to take in an ingredient which will give us a push. Holy love, the presence of Jesus in our lives, relieves us of seeking stimulation from any other source. He puts pep and go into us because love is the creative power of the universe.

And then, sometimes, life offers pain. Maybe all I need to do to deal with the hurting is turn to Jesus for his healing touch. Why should I go on and on trying to manage the pain by myself when he is ready and willing to give me some help? His shelves aren't empty and I don't need to go on aching.

The shopping list was as good as the speech notes. All I needed really was a reminder that wherever there is emptiness, he offers refilling; wherever there is longing, he stands by with gifts. If I use up what I have, he will replenish, for he is the eternal storehouse, never in short supply. And every day is Double Coupon Day. I receive double for what I have, redemption of my little for his much, a miracle for my loaves and fishes. He is the Alpha and the Omega. He is Lord and Savior. Amen.

Verses for Prayer

"If any man is thirsty, let him come to me! Let the man come and drink who believes in me" (Jn 7:37).

"Out of his infinite glory, may he give you the power through his Spirit for your hidden self to grow strong, so that Christ may live in your hearts through faith, and then,

124

planted in love and built on love, you will with all the saints have strength to grasp the breadth and the length, the height and the depth; until, knowing the love of Christ, which is beyond all knowledge, you are filled with the utter fullness of God" (Eph 3:16–20).

Conclusion

Now I am looking further at the little boy who gave his lunch to the Lord Jesus. The child almost surely waited around until the bread and fish were passed out and then, finally, ate his fill. It's likely he enjoyed lots more food than he would have if all he had eaten was his own original lunch. Perhaps the disciples even handed him a sack of leftovers to take home to his parents and his brothers and sisters. Probably he was so in awe of the Master who had turned his meager lunch into food for a multitude that he began to follow him and make his personal acquaintance. Possibly, as he grew, he became one of the bright lights in the spread of the wonderful Gospel of Jesus. Maybe he later lost his life in an act of bravery which showed outsiders new dimensions of the devotion which comes of truly *knowing* Jesus. I am sure that my own life, nearly two thousand years later, has been changed because of this long-ago child who gave all he had to his Lord. Giving what we have to Jesus for his miracle and his redemption has mind-boggling results. A person who is lost in a search for "meaning of life" might well find the deepest kind of importance in simply handing what he has over to God's power.

The same is true of each of us. Let me give what I have: anger, unforgiveness, misconceptions, prejudice, habits, willingness, imagination, creativity, experience, and whatever else I have yet to discover. They may not look like much. In fact, they probably seem mostly ugly, useless, and even destructive. But if I truly *give* them to Jesus, there is no end of wonder at what he will do with them. I may give either willingly or in fear and trembling, but help me, Lord, to truly let go and allow your hands to accept whatever I have to offer.

Just as the gifts of my loaves and fishes had ongoing results, so does this very *act* of giving. The boy's lunch sack was empty when he handed his loaves and fishes to Jesus. But our sacks appear never to run dry. All of the "gifts" we offer to our Lord seem to have tails and trains behind them. New anger and new unforgivenesses pop up. Old habits, long buried, come out in the open. New situations promise that prejudice can always rear its ungodly head. Habits form, someone told me, in any three-week period. Sometimes it takes much longer than that to root them out. However, the practice of offering-to-the-Lord is its own kind of habit, productive instead of debilitating. We all need to learn ways to strengthen the habit of giving whatever we have to Jesus.

Once when I was thinking about my many inadequacies and what to do with them, a picture came into my mind. It was of a large glass nearly full of rocks. I held up the glass, asking Jesus to fill it with his Spirit, his love, his very presence until it ran over and touched all the people in my world. He began to pour, but my glass had so many objects in it that there wasn't much room for the liquid of his Spirit. It ran over quickly, all right. Unhappily the liquid wasn't clear and lovely. The residue from all the rocks tainted it. As I picked them out, though, and gave them into his other hand, the glass could hold more and more of His goodness. Finally, when it filled to the top and began to run over the edges, it touched everyone around me with that pure and sparkling Spirit of God that drew them all to himself. It was a picture of what my life can be if I can develop the habit of offering all my hard and ugly things to him (and my joyous ones, too). Do help me to remember my vision whenever my days are full of unpleasantness of my own making, Lord, as well as when the skies are blue.

The little lad's lunch was turned into a miracle on a grassy slope in a long-ago land. I am not there with them in time or place. I am here in a country so different that there is little to link us together. Or is there? Yes, maybe there is. Jesus instituted the sacrament of the Eucharist on the night before he was betrayed, and it serves to connect all of us from that day to this. He was saying to us, "Through this holy experience, we are together in a way that is different from all others. I come to you in every area of your life and in every moment. But the altar of my sacrifice for you and yours to me is at the eucharistic table—the same now as it has always been." Day by day we can offer our little lunches, our crumbs, whatever we have that we do or do not want to keep for ourselves. And in that act of offering, we can see what we have given replaced by the body and blood of Jesus. The story in Scripture of the child's lunch had an ending—but it really didn't end. It has never ended. Neither will our gifts have an ending. The whole process is deliciously ongoing. We can go to the altar every day and let our Lord substitute the Spirit for the rocks, the baskets of food for our crumbs, the beautiful for the ugly. We can continue to "grow into his image" and become more and more whole until the moment when we will hear him say to us, "Well done, thou good and faithful servant."

Verses for Prayer
"So if the Son makes you free, you shall be free indeed" (Jn 8:36).